TUNE *your* FRENCH

The Top 10 Ways to Improve *your* Spoken French

Natalie Schorr

Mc
Graw
Hill

New York   Chicago   San Francisco   Lisbon   London   Madrid   Mexico City
Milan   New Delhi   San Juan   Seoul   Singapore   Sydney   Toronto

Library of Congress Cataloging-in-Publication Data

Schorr, Natalie Gillingham.
    Tune up your French : the top ten ways to improve your spoken French / Natalie Schorr.
        p.   cm.
    Includes index.
    ISBN 0-07-143230-2
    1. French language—Conversation and phrase books—English.   2. French
language—Textbooks for foreign speakers—English.   3. French language—Spoken
French.   I. Title.

PC2121.S417   2004
448.3′421—dc22   2004053859

Also in this series
Tune Up Your Spanish, *Mary McVey Gill and Brenda Wegmann*
Series editor: Natalie Schorr

    9 10 11 12 13 14 15 16 17 18 19 20 21 22 23 24   FGR/FGR   0 9

ISBN-13: 978-0-07-143229-0 (book and CD package)
ISBN-10:   0-07-143229-9 (book and CD package)
ISBN-13: 978-0-07-143230-6 (book only)
ISBN-10:   0-07-143230-2 (book only)

Interior design by Pamela Juárez

McGraw-Hill books are available at special quantity discounts to use as premiums and sales
promotions, or for use in corporate training programs. For more information, please write to
the Director of Special Sales, Professional Publishing, McGraw-Hill, Two Penn Plaza, New York,
NY 10121-2298. Or contact your local bookstore.

This book is printed on acid-free paper.

Contents

Acknowledgments

Special thanks go to the people who inspired me to write this book—the many acquaintances who so readily told me that they'd studied French but got stuck whenever they tried to say anything. I've always taught my students French without using any English. However, I knew I needed to find an engaging new approach for adults who felt frustrated. Idiomatic expressions often came to my mind as spoken by particular people and so I'm also indebted to my French role models of *l'art de vivre*.

I greatly appreciate the spring-term sabbatical from Phillips Academy that provided the time to get started on what became *Tune Up Your French*.

I am thankful to Christopher Brown at McGraw-Hill for his early interest in the book, and for his expert advice and many helpful suggestions along the way; to Julia Anderson Bauer for her fine work as Editorial Team Leader; and to Maki Wiering and Mireille Claret for their help in editing the manuscript.

My love and thanks go to my friends and family—particularly Sarah, Max, and Clare—for their encouragement, and to Mark, as always.

Introduction

When I'm introduced as a French teacher, people often respond by apologizing to me that they studied French for years but can't speak it. They say they would love to speak French but get stuck whenever they try to say something. This book is for them. It's not for beginners.

Tune Up Your French highlights *ce qui se dit*. It features the idioms that French people use every day but that most students who have studied French for three, four, or more years don't have on the tip of the tongue.

Consider the following expressions: "That sounds right." "It sounded as though you didn't mean it." "How does that sound?" "That sounds incredible." "It sounds as though he got it." "It doesn't sound as though you liked it." "Let me say it out loud to hear how it sounds." After tuning up your French you'll have a better sense of what sounds right in French.

You were born with the ability to speak French just as well as English, but once your brain becomes used to English you aren't spontaneously going to come up with French expressions by thinking in English. The context for *Tune Up Your French* is the connection between language and ways of thinking.

To connect language and culture *Tune Up Your French* will:

- include body language, such as *la bise*
- explore alternative meanings of *Merci* and *Je vous en prie*
- reveal the various ways to say *alors*
- tell you to say «*s'il vous plaît*» to get the attention of a salesperson in a store
- remind you to say «*Monsieur!*» instead of «*Garçon!*» to call a waiter
- reveal the unwritten rules about slang
- emphasize French expressions that have a certain *je ne sais quoi*
- show you how you can make your point in French by saying the opposite of what you mean
- give you a repertoire of *mots historiques*
- provide the *trucs* for demystifying the tricks of French

This approach will help you if you studied French grammar and vocabulary but felt as though you couldn't say anything. You take advantage of the French you already have as you develop your ear for spoken French. The approach encourages you to continue with French by going to French movies, listening to the radio and television in French, learning French songs, traveling in France and the francophone world, and talking with French-speaking people.

The Ten French Tune-Ups

First, in "The Zazie Effect," you will review ten characteristics of French pronunciation and intonation that apply to all of the tune-ups. On the CD, tips on French pronunciation and intonation are interspersed among the exercises.

The "Quick Fixes" section provides expressions that build your confidence and give you an informal preview of what's to come.

Not only can you say something in French but you can have fun doing it.

Each of the ten major tune-ups suggests a different way in which you can improve your spoken French. Each section includes top ten lists related to the same concept. The lists contain expressions you hear in France every day. I chose the idioms that I'd enjoyed learning because they were lively, they were practical, and they revealed a French way of thinking.

A list of twenty questions at the beginning of each tune-up serves as both a diagnostic self-test and a taster for the chapter. Another twenty questions follow the chapter to give you practice with what you've learned. Answers for the latter appear in the Answer Key.

"Tune-Up 1: Nonverbal Cues, Sound Effects, and Interjections" shows how you can communicate in French with body language and sounds before you even start dealing with words. It demonstrates how meaning can change according to the sounds you make in French and explores the connection between sounds and words through interjections. Some of the interjections are actual words and some of them are just onomatopoeic noises, but they function the same way.

"Tune-Up 2: Manners" demonstrates that the French have their own way of being polite and shows you how to be polite when speaking French. Polite expressions are called magic words with good reason, and they are particularly powerful in French when used the French way.

"Tune-Up 3: Idioms to Go" shows you how to use one-word, two-word, and three-word idioms that make you sound as though you know your way around. This section provides a guide to fillers and other short expressions that make you sound more like a native French speaker.

"Tune-Up 4: Practical French" highlights hands-on French, helping you with what to say in a store and at the train station so that you can handle everyday situations with aplomb. What the

French actually say in a given situation can be quite different from what Americans would say.

"Tune-Up 5: Table Talk" presents gastronomic correctness as the French form of political correctness. Learning French while eating French food is one of the most enjoyable methods of learning by doing. You also remember vocabulary better when you associate it with taste.

"Tune-Up 6: Conversation Starters" shows you how to get the French—or for that matter anyone else—to talk to you. Learning a language isn't as much fun if you can't get people to talk with you. There are models and subjects for different kinds of questions to ask in French. As you continue with French, questions will become an increasingly valuable tool. If you can ask the right question you can open a conversation.

"Tune-Up 7: Slang and Other Kinds of French" demystifies slang by sorting it out, giving you tips on what slang you can use and what you can't. Not understanding slang is a common and often intimidating problem if you aren't familiar with French culture, but slang can be fun to use if you know what's appropriate.

"Tune-Up 8: Attitude" presents the sort of French expressions that Americans usually think of as transmitting a French attitude. The nuances of these French expressions can make us look at something from a new angle. Sometimes they seem to provide what our own language is missing. Through working with both literal meanings and informal connotations you have an idea of what it means to see and feel things the French way.

"Tune-Up 9: Wit" shows you how to play with the French language so that you will care about it as much as the French do. You learn techniques for expressing the wit that springs from an ironic outlook.

"Tune-Up 10: Improvisation" brings you French quotations, some famous ones, some representative ones, and many just my personal favorites. You'll see how French writers have used French quotations as a starting point for their own writing. Finally, you'll use the quotations to help you improvise. You gain a sense of *forme et fond*, style and substance, as you express yourself. French *bons mots* will help you to understand French culture.

Appendix A includes *trucs* to guide you on the slippery path of misleading cognates, *faux amis*, and tricky French structures. You will see, for example, how the subjunctive is used in simple sentences in everyday conversation. There is no attempt to cover all of basic grammar, though, as this is a book for people who have already studied French and can consult a French grammar book and French dictionary for reference if necessary. Appendix B consists of ten common idioms, each of which is presented along with ten variations. These idioms have the effect of multiplying your active vocabulary. Finally, an Answer Key is provided for the questions appearing at the end of each chapter.

All of the chapters together will prepare you to move ahead with spoken French by linking literal meanings and connotative meanings, language, and culture. You will find that your fluency evolves and that the French language itself also evolves. French isn't a packaged product that can be delivered by a method in a fixed amount of time. These tune-ups will help you find your French voice.

The Zazie Effect

Putting all of the features of spoken French together we have the Zazie effect. In his novel *Zazie dans le métro*, Raymond Queneau plays with the way whole utterances sound when they run together, and he writes them the way they sound—as though they are one long word.

The first word in *Zazie dans le métro* is a question: *Doukipudonktan. (D'où est-ce qu'ils puent donc tant?)* "Why do they stink so much?" Queneau treats the spoken expression *doukipudonktan* as a unit that results particularly from three characteristics of French—elision, liaison, and lack of stress. These factors come into play in making the words of sentences sound as though they run together as one.

TOP TEN Examples of Zaziefication in Conversation

1. **Keskitapri?** (*Qu'est-ce qui t'a pris?*) What's gotten into you?

2. **Jensépamwa.** (*Je ne sais pas, moi.*) I dunno.

3. **Satplé?** (*Ça te plaît?*) Do you like it?

4. **Pamal.** (*Pas mal.*) Not bad.

5. **Satdérange?** (*Ça te dérange?*) Is this bothering you?

6. **Padproblèm.** (*Pas de problème.*) No problem.

7. **Kesketuraconte?** (*Qu'est-ce que tu racontes?*) What are you talking about?

8. **Laisstombé.** (*Laisse tomber.*) Forget it.

9. **Commensasfé?** (*Comment ça se fait?*) How could that be?

10. **Méssénormal.** (*Mais c'est normal.*) It's only to be expected.

TOP TEN — Aspects of French Pronunciation and Intonation

While Queneau wrote *Zazie dans le métro* in familiar French, his basic observations about the sound of French hold true for spoken French in general. Whole French expressions are uttered as connected sounds.

This is not a complete description of French phonetics but an attempt to highlight ten essential features of French pronunciation that contrast with English. It starts with the smallest unit, the letter, and moves up to the pronunciation of groups of words and the intonation of sentences.

1. Pronouncing French Takes More Energy Than Pronouncing English

Since French and English have the same alphabet, you need to make a particular effort to let go of the way the letters are pronounced in English in order to say them the French way instead. Non-native speakers of French have to pay particular attention to the *r* and the *u*, for example.

The French *r* and *u* are considered the most different letter sounds for native speakers of English. Pronouncing the French *r* nonchalantly can seem like trying to be subtle when you gargle.

The French *r* is in your throat whereas the English *r* is in your mouth. You actually do have to gargle to understand the location of the French *r*, which is closer to the pronunciation of the German *ch* (as in "Bach") than to the English *r*.

French vowels are tight and self-contained, whereas English vowels tend to be diphthongs in disguise, with one vowel sound sliding into another. Take care to pronounce the French vowels as single sounds. Compare the gliding vowels of English with the energetic French vowels in these examples: "ray" with *ré*, "see" with *si*, "oh" with *ô*, "you" and *où*, "Jules" (pronounced like "jewels") with *Jules*.

The French *u* is a tight and closed vowel. Practice it by shaping and energizing your mouth. First you make the sound *ee* as in "week." Then round your lips and move them forward as though to pronounce *oo*, as in "boo" or "Yule," but without actually making an *oo* sound. Finally, make the French *u* sound from the same tight position but farther back in your mouth.

2. Use Your Nose as Well as Your Mouth and Throat

When *m* or *n* ends a word or is followed by a consonant other than *m* or *n*, the preceding vowel is nasalized and the *m* or *n* is not pronounced. It's because of the nasal sounds in French that the word *instinct*, as spoken in French, would be unrecognizable to an American who didn't speak French.

Use both your nose and mouth for the nasal vowels.

The French nasal vowels are:

1. an, en, am, em   plan, enfant, tambour, emploi

2. in, ain, im, ein   vin, bain, faim, timbre, hein

3. on, om   non, combien

4. un, um   lundi, parfum

5. oin   point

3. In French, Don't Expect to Hear What You See at the End of a Word

You need to know not only how to pronounce French letters but also when to pronounce them and when not to. Most final consonants are not pronounced in French. Here are a few examples.

TOP TEN French Words That Have Unpronounced Final Letters

1. **les bœufs** (no final *fs*) steers

2. **le jus** (no *s*) juice

3. **un pas** (no *s*) step

4. **mais** (no *s*) but

5. **monsieur** (no *r*) sir

6. **le pot** (no *t*) pot

7. **le respect** (no *ct*) respect

8. **le tabac** (no *c*) tobacco

9. **le nid** (no *d*) nest

10. **trop** (no *p*) too much

A few words do have final consonants that are pronounced, however. *C* is pronounced in *lac* and *sac* but not in *blanc* and *estomac*. *F*, *l*, and *r* are usually pronounced, as in *neuf*, *mal*, *car*, and *pour*.

4. French Syllables Start with Consonant Sounds and End with Vowel Sounds

Since French syllables end with vowel sounds, the consonants which may look as though they end a syllable actually start the sound of the next syllable. *Il a fini* becomes *i—la—fi-ni* with open syllables, and then with liaison, it's *Ilafini*. Compare the syllables of *Elle a raison* with the English equivalent, "She's right."

The French syllables are: *E/lla/rai/son*.
The English syllables are: She's/right.

5. In French, There's No Pause Between Words or Syllables

In French *l'enchaînement* and *la liaison* link one sound to the next. *L'enchaînement* refers to linking or chaining the final sound of one syllable to the beginning of the next.

La liaison means that you also pronounce some sounds that would not otherwise be pronounced. French pronunciation can vary according to what sounds good to the French ear. The French put a lot of stock in euphony, pronouncing normally unpronounced letters when they will add smoothness. In front of a vowel or a silent *h*, you usually pronounce a consonant that normally wouldn't be pronounced.

Some examples of French sounds that change because of *liaison* are:

- final *s* or *x* of an article or adjective: *les̬amis, trois̬élèves, six̬étudiants*
- final *t* or *d* both sound like *t*: *un petit̬hôtel, un grand̬hôtel*
- final *n* of a nasal vowel: *un̬hôpital, son̬amie*
- *s* between a subject pronoun and a verb sounds like a *z*: *nous̬avons, elles̬habitent*
- *t* in inversion: *mangent-̬ils* (and with an added *t* in: *a-t-̬il*)

You *never* have the liaison, though, in the following cases:

- between a proper name and a verb: *Jean a*
- after *et* (and): *un homme et une femme*

6. In French, Contractions Are Required

In English, contractions are optional and informal. You can say either "I'd say so" or "I would say so," but in French there are rules for *élision*. A word's final vowel officially disappears in front of a word starting with a vowel or silent *h*, an *h muet*. You must say *Ce n'est pas l'amie d'Yves* rather than *Ce ne est pas la amie de Yves*.

There's no elision, though, with *h aspiré* in words such as *les haricots verts* and *la hache* and *le huit*, and there's no elision in the case of the two words *onze* and *oui*: *le onze*; *le oui*.

7. French Keeps a Steady Rhythm

In French each syllable has the same stress, but in English the accent varies. French syllables are said to have no stress, although it sounds and feels, to a native speaker of English, as though the stress falls on the last syllable of a French word or on the last syllable of a group of words.

This is why French poetry has *alexandrins* while English has iambic pentameter. In the *alexandrin*, the classic French line of poetry, each line has twelve syllables and each syllable has the same stress.

In English, accents naturally fall on different syllables in different words. Compare the English and French pronunciations of the words "revenue" and *revenue*; "important" and *important*; "camaraderie" and *camaraderie*. Occasionally in French you will hear a normally unaccented part of a word accented for emphasis: *C'est IM-peccable. C'était IN-croyable.*

8. French Segments Sentences in Order to Accentuate a Particular Meaning

French segments sentences for emphasis, tending to break the rhythm rather than add an accent to a word. English highlights words for emphasis, tending to move the accent around from word to word within the same sentence for emphasis.

Compare the ways French and English can highlight some different possible meanings of a sentence:

Il regarde mes tableaux.	He is looking at my paintings.
Il regarde mes tableaux, lui.	**He** is looking at my paintings.
Mais si. Il regarde mes tableaux.	He **is** looking at my paintings.
Il les regarde, mes tableaux.	He's **looking** at my paintings.
Mes tableaux à moi, il les regarde.	He's looking at **my** paintings.

9. In French, Statements Become Questions Through Change in Intonation

In conversation, any statement can become a question if your voice goes up at the end. The most common kind of question in spoken French is written like a statement with a question mark at the end.

Here are some examples of questions in informal conversation:

Tu ne veux pas?	Don't you want to?
Tu n'as pas compris?	Don't you get it?

10. French Intonation Creates Meanings

How something is said creates meaning just as much as what is said. This is true in both French and English, but it can be done in a different way in French. The CD will show how *oui* and *non* and *oh là là* can be said in different ways to create particular meanings. As you learn to use French intonation you will understand implied meanings and innuendo, perhaps the most difficult aspects of learning to speak another language.

All ten of these features of French pronunciation apply to all ten of the Tune-Ups. Listen for them in the expressions you hear on the CD and keep them in mind as you practice the expressions in this book.

Quick Fixes

If you're impatient to get started speaking in French, it's better to have some things to say right away rather than to think you can't say anything at all. The reason so many people feel they can't say anything in French is that they're afraid. They have tried to learn a lot all at once without having a base of real French expressions that they can produce easily. I believe, with strong anecdotal evidence, that anyone who can say at least 100 authentic French expressions really well will eventually become fluent in French. Once you can say a few expressions that sound French you will keep learning more. Pick a few more you would like to be able to say, think about why they sound French, and notice specifically what you like about them. Have fun. You'll remember what you want to say and you'll enjoy doing it.

Ten Top Ten Lists of Authentic French Expressions

TOP TEN Ways to Show Enthusiasm

1. **Génial!** Brilliant!

2. **Bravo!** Bravo!

3. **Chapeau!** Well done!

4. **Épatant!** Splendid!

5. **Formidable!** Terrific!

6. **Impeccable!** Wonderful!

7. **Magnifique!** Great!

8. **Super!** Fabulous!

9. **Extra!** Fantastic!

10. **Chouette!** Cool! (Familiar; *une chouette* is an owl.)

TOP TEN Ways to Say "Yes"

1. **Eh oui.** Guess so.

2. **Entendu, oui.** Right.

3. **D'accord.** All right.

4. **Je ne dis pas non.** I accept.

5. **Bien sûr que oui.** Of course.

6. **Ouais.** Yeah.

7. **Si!** Yes, on the contrary.

8. **Volontiers.** Yes. With pleasure.

9. **Mais oui.** Sure.

10. **Ah, ça, oui.** You can say that again.

TOP TEN Ways to Say "No"

1. **Je crois que non.** I don't think so.

2. **Moi, non.** Not me.

3. **Non.** No.

4. **Bien sûr que non.** Definitely not.

5. **Ah, ça, non!** I'm not going along with that!

6. **Non, merci!** No thank you! How could you imagine that I would!

7. **Non, mais dites donc...** No. Come off it . . .

8. **Non, alors!** That's going too far.

9. **Alors, non!** No way!

10. **Non, non, et non!** No. And that's final.

TOP TEN Ways to Slow Down the Conversation

1. **Hein?** Huh?

2. **Comment?** What was that?

3. **Pardon?** Excuse me?

4. **Vous disiez?** You were saying?

5. **Je n'ai pas compris.** I didn't understand.

6. **Répétez s'il vous plaît.** Could you repeat that please?

7. **Qu'est-ce que vous avez dit?** What did you say?

8. **Je ne suis pas sûr d'avoir compris.** I'm not sure I understood.

9. **Plus lentement s'il vous plaît.** Speak more slowly please.

10. **Pourriez-vous me l'écrire s'il vous plaît?** Could you write that down for me please?

TOP TEN Terms of Endearment

1. **Mon petit chou.** My little cabbage.

2. **Mon chéri; ma chérie.** My beloved.

3. **Mon petit lapin.** My little rabbit.

4. **Mon nounours.** My teddy bear.

5. **Mon amour.** My love.

6. **Ma cocotte.** My hen. My sweetie.

7. **Ma bibiche.** My doe. My honey.

8. **Mon ange.** My angel.

9. **Ma bobonne.** My missus. My dear.

10. **Ma puce.** My flea. My pet.

TOP TEN Ways to Describe Someone

1. **C'est un bon vivant.** He lives it up.

2. **C'est un chic type.** He's a nice guy.

3. **Il/Elle a le cœur sur la main.** He/She is generous.

4. **Il/Elle a toujours le mot pour rire.** He/She likes to joke around.

5. **C'est une femme de tête.** She's an intellectual.

6. **Il/Elle a un poil dans la main.** He/She is lazy.

7. **C'est un numéro.** He's/She's a character. (**C'est un drôle de numéro.** He's/She's quite a character.)

8. **C'est un boute-en-train.** He/She is the life of the party.

9. **C'est une vraie girouette.** He/She changes his/her mind according to which way the wind is blowing. (literally, is a weather vane)

10. **C'est une bonne poire.** He/She is a sucker.

TOP TEN   Abbreviations for Talking About Education

1. **Ils vont à la fac.** (*faculté*) They're going to class. (at a university; i.e., the Faculty of Arts and Sciences)

2. **Elle est prof.** (*professeur*) She's a teacher.

3. **Ils passent le bac.** (*baccalauréat*) They're taking the baccalaureate exam. (after high school)

4. **On fait des maths.** (*mathématiques*) We're studying math.

5. **Elle a une dissert.** (*dissertation*) She has a paper to write.

6. **Je n'ai pas de dico.** (*dictionnaire*) I don't have a dictionary.

7. **On apprend la géo.** (*géographie*) We're learning geography.

8. **Ils ont une interro.** (*interrogation*) They have a test.

9. **On va au labo.** (*laboratoire*) We're going to the lab.

10. **Elle fait sciences-po.** (*sciences-politiques*) She's studying political science.

TOP TEN Slang Expressions That Will Never Get You into Trouble

1. **J'ai fait une gaffe.** I made a mistake.

2. **J'ai un rencard.** (*J'ai un rendez-vous.*) I have a date. I'm meeting someone.

3. **On va demander au flic.** Let's ask the cop.

4. **On va prendre un pot?** Shall we get something to drink? (in a café or bar)

5. **Je prends la bagnole.** I'm taking the car.

6. **Il est branché.** He's in the know. (plugged in)

7. **C'est marrant.** That's funny.

8. **J'aime bien ce bouquin.** I really like this/that book.

9. **C'est un tube.** It's a hit song.

10. **Vous avez un truc pour l'ouvrir?** Do you have something to open it with? (*Un truc*, a thingamajig, is useful if you can't think of the right word. So is *un machin*.)

TOP TEN French Euphemisms

1. **C'est une femme d'un certain âge.** She's no longer as young as she would like to be. (Literally, it's a woman of a certain age.)

2. **Il nous a quittés.** He died. (Literally, he left us.) Also: *Il a disparu.* (Literally, he disappeared.) Also: *Le Cercle des poètes disparus.* (*The Dead Poets Society*).

3. **Elle est allée au petit coin.** She went to the bathroom. (Literally, she went to the little corner.)

4. **Il a remercié ses employés.** He fired his employees. (Literally, he thanked his employees.)

5. **Elle a la langue bien pendue.** She will talk your head off. (Literally, she has a well-hung tongue.)

6. **Il brillait par son absence.** He was conspicuously absent. (Literally, he shone by his absence.)

7. **Allez voir ailleurs si j'y suis.** Go fly a kite. (Literally, go look somewhere else to see if I'm there.)

8. **C'est une personne un peu forte.** He/She is a bit stout. (Literally, he/she is a little strong.)

9. **Il se regarde passer.** He's vain. (Literally, he watches himself go by.)

10. **Ils peignent la girafe.** It's busywork. (Literally, they're combing the giraffe.)

TOP TEN Things to Say to Make a French Meal Less Expensive

1. **Une carafe d'eau, s'il vous plaît.** A jug of water, please. (Tap water is usually drinkable, if you want to save money by not ordering mineral water.)

2. **La réserve du patron.** The house wine. (A self-respecting establishment usually has a very good inexpensive house wine. This excellent expression deserves to be better known and used frequently.)

3. **Un vin du pays.** A local wine. (This is a good euphemism for ordering a cheap wine because it's a good idea to order the local wine anyway.)

4. **Un petit vin.** A local wine. Inexpensive but good. (*Un petit vin* is not necessarily pejorative even though it suggests its opposite, *un grand vin*, a great wine.)

5. **Une pression.** A (draught) beer.

6. **On va manger au bar.** We'll eat at the counter. (If you can eat or drink at the counter it's usually cheaper.)

7. **On va prendre le menu.** We'll take the fixed price meal (less expensive if you want a full meal).

8. **On prendra la formule.** We'll take the combination. (This is the same idea as *le menu*; a couple of courses are combined at a special price—first course and main course or main course and dessert.)

9. **Vous avez un plat du jour?** Do you have a special? (It may not be the least expensive main course, but it will probably be especially good and less expensive than the regular menu.)

10. **Un dessert pour deux. C'est possible? On peut partager?** Could we possibly share a dessert? (There's no harm in asking if it's possible to share a dessert at an informal meal.)

Bonus: **On peut faire la vaisselle?** Can we do the dishes?

Nonverbal Cues, Sound Effects, and Interjections

Make the Most of Body Language and Simple Expressions

Preview

1. When counting on your fingers in French, which finger do you start with?

2. Does a smile mean the same thing in France as it does in the United States?

3. What's the significance of keeping your hands out of your pockets?

4. How should you interpret a pout in response to a question?

5. Do the French tend to stand closer to or farther away from each other than Americans do when having a conversation?

6. How would you gesture that someone is drunk?

7. When do you knock on a closed door?

8. What gesture indicates that someone is nuts?

9. What gesture indicates skepticism?

10. How is a French handshake different from an American one?

11. If you are not very familiar with French culture, with whom could you initiate cheek kissing?

12. What gesture expresses indifference?

13. What sound expresses indifference?

14. Is there a way to say "splish splash" in French?

15. Does the French expression *oh là là* mean the same thing in French as it does in English?

16. What sound would you make in French if you stubbed your toe but not badly enough to swear?

17. What do the French say instead of "whoopsie-daisy" when helping a child over a puddle?

18. What sound do the French make to silence someone who might otherwise wake a sleeping baby?

19. Do the French shout *Encore!* if they like a performance?

20. How would you say "Well, well . . ." in French?

You can improve your spoken French just by learning French body language. The key to using French effectively is the ability to communicate with gestures and sounds as well as words.

Observe how the French say what they say. Do they make eye contact? What tone of voice, pitch, speed of delivery, and facial expressions do they use? Are there pauses in their conversations? How do people stand, and how close are they to each other? What kind of gestures do they make? In what ways do they touch each other? What do they smell like? What do they like to eat? What style of clothes do they have and how do they wear them?

Communication involves understanding what people really mean as well as understanding the literal meaning of their words. Everyone thinks about the role of nonverbal communication when going for an interview. It's important to remember this also when learning French so that you think of language as more than just words.

TOP TEN Kinds of French Nonverbal Communication

1. Mime

Mime is not the typical type of nonverbal communication because it is conscious. You can point, as politely as possible, and use props to communicate. You can produce a map and a pencil when asking directions or use a pad and pencil to draw a picture of what you can't say. Or you can just act out your idea. While mime is international, there are a few points to keep in mind in French.

The hands provide excellent props for mime. You use the thumb rather than the index finger to indicate "one" when counting on your fingers. The index finger is two, and so forth.

You can use your hand to mime a telephone. Bring your hand next to your ear with the thumb and little finger extended. This means *On se téléphone.*

Use both hands to signal to the waiter that you'd like the check. You pretend to write on the palm of one hand with the other hand. *L'addition s'il vous plaît.*

2. Eye Contact

The French tend to like direct eye contact, except for staring. Eye contact establishes complicity. For example, people who don't know each other and would not normally speak with each other may catch each other's eye and raise an eyebrow to share their amusement at an absurd situation. If you can catch another driver's eye in traffic, he or she will usually let you into a line. If you look a waiter in the eye, he or she may take you more seriously as a customer. People in small stores generally like you to make eye contact with them briefly and to say *Bonjour, monsieur* or *Bonjour, madame* before you say what you want.

3. Facial Expressions

Smiles, pouts, and flirtatious looks convey messages without words. When a smile is not prompted by anything in particular, the French may see it as a sign of stupidity rather than of friendliness. Or worse, they may consider it *un sourire de circonstance*, an ingratiating smile. The French tend to smile when there is a reason to smile. A smile can thank someone for a service or express empathy. The French tend not to smile for a passport photo. A French smile is intended to show that you have made a connection. You don't need to know someone before you smile, but you will have made polite eye contact. The French may speak disparagingly of the unfocused *sourire américain*, but they like *un vrai sourire*, a real smile: for example, an amused smile or a kind smile. A smile remains, in any case, one of the most positive forms of international body language. It definitely draws a warmer response than a blank look or a frown.

When a response to a question is a two-second pout, it usually means, "This calls for reflection. I'm thinking for a moment before giving my reply. " It does *not* give a clue that the reply will be negative. The response when it comes may be positive. A pout can sometimes indicate *je m'enfous*, a lack of preference. But wait and see.

To many French women as well as French men, the sexual look or positive comment about physical appearance that (usually) a man directs toward (usually) a woman in a social situation, on the street, or in the office is taken as flattery rather than as a cause for offense. American annoyance in a similar situation may be considered puritanical rather than enlightened. Increasingly, however, the French show a range of reactions to this kind of look. The look is now often considered inappropriate and demeaning in France too. Which is it? It may depend upon the beholder, the beheld, and the situation.

4. Posture

On the whole the French seem to have better posture than Americans, even though it's not as good as that of the Senegalese, Indians, or Egyptians. Standing up straight and keeping your hands out of your pockets can indicate self-respect and respect for others in France.

5. Use of Space

A French person may prefer to stand very close to someone while carrying on a conversation in order to speak softly for privacy. An American may feel his or her space invaded by the closeness and then step back while speaking relatively loudly—even if it means that others can overhear the conversation.

Similarly, Americans may think that tables in French restaurants are too close together. But the French consider that you should talk quietly enough so that you can't be heard at the next table.

6. Gestures

In France, always knock on a closed door before opening it. Knocking on a closed door—*toc toc*—is a polite way of announcing your entry, whether or not anyone is on the other side to hear you.

A pout—*bof*—with a shrug, the elbows close to the body, hands palms-up and wider apart than the elbows means "So what? Who cares?" This is a standard expression of *je-m'en-foutisme*. (The pout that goes with *Je m'en fous* became an established French attitude, *le je-m'en-foutisme*, "I don't-give-a-damnism." It's the opposite of *Qu'en dira-t-on?* and *le qu'en-dira-t-on*, the concern with what people will think.)

Tapping your forehead with your index finger or making small circles with your index finger touching the side of your forehead—rather than circling your finger near your ear—indicates that someone has done something crazy. *Ça ne va pas, non?*

Pulling down your lower eyelid with your index finger indicates disbelief and skepticism. *Mon œil.* "My eye. A likely story!"

You can indicate that you think someone or something is boring by stroking your chin as though stroking a beard or by rolling your eyes. These gestures go with the slang expression *la barbe*.

If you want to point out that someone is drunk, you can do this by pretending to grab your nose with your fist and then screwing it to the side.

Three shakes of the hand from the wrist indicate that you had a close call. *Je l'ai échappé belle.* "I was scared there for a moment."

7. Touch

Notice the way people touch each other in France. Obviously everyone has a different way. But in general, in terms of asexual greetings among friends, there's probably more cheek contact and less hugging than Americans are used to.

Among couples there may be more nonchalance. If you see a couple kissing on a park bench, this may be considered an assumption of respect for privacy that allows for detached obliviousness, rather than a public display of affection. There's tenderness in a light touch and perhaps as much face touching and hair stroking as kissing on the lips. In general, people seem to touch each others' arms more frequently, and one sees more public touching among older couples as well as among younger ones.

There's also a gentle sense of smell and touch regarding food. At home, the French may lightly squeeze fruit to see if it's ripe and pat the bread to see if it's fresh. The reason people who work at open-air markets are strict about not letting you touch the fruit is that everyone wants to do it, just to check. They can tell you from their own gentle touch just when the peaches should be eaten.

A kiss on both cheeks, *la bise*, is a sign of affection among family members and good friends. It takes place between children, between a child and an adult, between women, between a man and a woman, and sometimes between men. Basically everyone does it, and in France it is about the same thing as being on a first-name basis with someone in the United States. First-name use is less common than in the United States, while cheek kissing is more common. Remember that it's asexual. Do not initiate cheek kissing, however, and do not misconstrue it as more than a pleasant formality. Start with the right cheek. Plan for one on each side, but since cheek kissing can involve two, three, or four kisses, be ready to improvise. Think of it as an air kiss.

A French handshake, *une poignée de main*, stops short of a full American handshake. Think of the handshake as a soft grasp, up and down once, and release. Usually people shake hands lightly with everyone present when saying hello and good-bye. They do this with groups of friends on social occasions and with colleagues at work. Sometimes there may be only a few minutes between the hello handshake and the good-bye handshake.

8. Smell

The French have a refined sense of smell, as evidenced by the vast number of delicately nuanced perfumes. Body odor, however, is a sensitive subject between the French and Americans. What to Americans is "not dealing with body odor" may be to the French "accepting the natural smells of the body." What to the French may be "an obsessive preoccupation with masking the odors of the body" may be to Americans "excellent hygiene." Obviously the French don't all smell the same any more than Americans do. But the French, in general, seem to have more acceptance of and even affection for the body's natural odors.

9. Taste

Snails? Frog's legs? Calf brains? Sorrel? Lemon verbena? In general, the French enjoy a larger range of food than do Americans. They respect the freshness of fruits and vegetables and like to eat them only in season, probably more so than most Americans.

Taste can depend on context, too. To fully appreciate a French meal, the French progress through the different courses following a definite order. Sometimes tasting can be a separate stage of eating or drinking. For example, the French often taste a wine before drinking it.

The French usually don't like the taste of processed foods, and they reject low-fat foods if they don't taste good. Many of them protest the influx of fast-food places such as McDonald's, but others apparently like the convenience they provide.

10. Clothes or Lack Thereof

French clothes have a closer fit than American clothes. To Americans, French men and women can often look as though they are wearing their clothes too tight. A style that can look conventional to a French eye can look intentionally provocative to an American one, just as bright colors, logos, and shirts hanging out can look casual to Americans while appearing unsubtle and even vulgar to the French.

Most French people appear slim to Americans, and lots of Americans look fat to the French. And the French who have older or wider bodies than others don't as often feel the need to cover them as Americans do. A normal seventy-year-old French woman can appear self-confident and comfortable in a bikini or even topless on the beach. On the other hand, the same seventy-year-old woman would not think of entering a cathedral wearing shorts and a T-shirt. Her philosophy would be to have *une tenue correcte*, to be appropriately dressed.

Sound Effects

Sound effects are a special kind of nonverbal communication. They communicate meaning without actually being words. Even when noises, such as the crowing of a rooster, are the same in both French and English, the sounds that the different languages use to represent the same noise—*cocorico* and cock-a-doodle-doo—are different. While it's not particularly important to know the French spellings of these sounds, it's crucial to realize that the English language is not the default language for sounds. Displacing the water in the bathtub makes a *flic flac* as legitimately as a "splish splash." *Toc toc* is "knock knock," and *tic-tac* is "tick tock."

The actual noise that's heard may of course vary from culture to culture. *Pin-pon*, the distinctive noise of *la voiture de pompiers*, is quite different from the siren of the American fire engine.

TOP TEN French Noises

1. **Flic flac!** Splish splash!

2. **Glouglou!** Glug-glug!

3. **Vroum!** Va va voom!

4. **Floc!** Plop!

5. **Dring!** Rrring!

6. **Pif! Paf!** Bang! Bang!

7. **Pim! Pam! Poum!** Bing! Bang! Boom!

8. **Pschitt!** or **Pscht!** (sound of effervescence; a soft drink opening; it's said very quickly and pronounced "psheet")

9. **Tic-tac.** Tick tock.

10. **Pin-pon!** (sound of the horn of the French fire truck)

Interjections

Interjections are sudden short utterances, often not really words. Sounds that aren't words are part of communication, just as sound itself provides another dimension of communication. The way something is said—how it sounds—often means more than what is said. Interjections can help you get a feeling for French sounds.

"Oh la la!" in English is different from *oh là là* in French. The American "oh la la!" can mean "Wow! That's really a fancy looking French dress." The French *oh là là* has more options, but that kind of "Wow!" isn't one of them.

To express surprise and pleasure you could say: *Oh là là... Quelle surprise!*

If you're shocked you might say: *Oh là là... C'est la catastrophe!*

If you can't believe your eyes you might say: *Oh là là là là... Mais c'est incroyable!*

While thinking of what he wants to say the Frenchman murmurs *euh...* (not "um"). If he stubs his toe he'll yelp *Aïe!* ("Ouch!"). *Encore* is a French word, but the French don't yell *Encore!* if they want an encore after a performance. The French expression for that is *Bis!*

TOP TEN Basic Interjections

1. **Aïe!** (pain)

2. **Zut!** (anger)

3. **Bof** (indifference)

4. **Hein?** (incomprehension)

5. **Youpi!** (excitement)

6. **Chut!** (impatience; desire for silence)

7. **Ouf!** (relief)

8. **Ah!** (surprise)

9. **Euh...** (hesitation)

10. **Bis!** (enjoyment of a performance)

Hop-là

If you watch a French parent holding a child's hand to help her jump over a puddle the parent will invariably say, *Hop-là*. If you can say *hop-là* when crossing a puddle, *motus* when telling a secret, *pharamineux* when you have all the aces, *turlututu* when someone stretches the truth, and *tope-là* when slapping someone's hand as you make a deal—then you will deserve to hear *Pchch*.

Children say *Chiche* when they are daring each other to do something risky. *Beurk* is the cartoon language for "Yuck." *Allez, ouste!* or just *Ouste!* is "Go on. Get going." The French have adopted the Italian interjection, *Basta!* for "Enough!" and also have their own variation, *Baste*, to indicate disdainful indifference: "Never mind. So what? Who cares?"

Some old-fashioned sounding expressions such as *Hélas!* to indicate regret and *Peste!* to indicate surprise may still be heard, but now usually with an ironic tone.

TOP TEN Advanced Interjections

1. **Hop-là!** Whoopsie-daisy!

2. **Motus!** (**Motus et bouche cousue**) Don't breathe a word and seal your lips. (complicity)

3. **Baste!** Never mind. (indifference)

4. **Pharamineux!** (admiration)

5. **Turlututu!** (skepticism)

6. **Chiche!** I dare you! (provocation)

7. **Tope-là.** (acceptance)

8. **Pchch!** (ironic admiration)

9. **Beurk!** (disgust)

10. **Ouste!** Scram!

Allez, va!

In the expression *Allez, va!* the second-person plural imperative and second-person singular imperative become an interjection together. As a transition from French noises to French words, consider the following list of ten expressions, all spelled as variations on one verb, *aller*, "to go," in its three imperative forms: *Va! Allons! Allez!* Interjections with *aller* function exactly the same way as interjections that are just sounds, such as *Pchch!*

Other verbs can double as interjections as well. *Tenir* yields *Tiens!* which can mean "Hey!" or "What do you know?" or "What a surprise to see you!" Then there's also *Tiens, tiens*, which means "Well, well" or "Fancy seeing you here." *Tenez!* can mean "Wait a second!"

From the verb *dire* comes the interjection *Dites donc!* (also *Dis donc!*) meaning "Hey there!" or "Hey you!" or sometimes "Can you believe it?" *Dites* alone can be "By the way . . ." *Dites, si on allait voir ce film, ce soir?* "By the way, how about going to see that movie tonight?"

TOP TEN   Interjections from the Imperative of *aller*

1. **Va.** You'll get over it.

2. **Va donc!** What do you think you're doing!

3. **Allons!** Come on! Go on!

4. **Allons, allons.** Come on. Don't get upset.

5. **Allons bon!** What's wrong *now*?

6. **Allons donc!** You've got to be kidding. Give me a break.

7. **Allez!** OK then.

8. **Allez, allez.** Keep moving.

9. **Allez, va!** Go on!

10. **Allez la France!** Go France! Come on France! (a sports cheer)

Rehearsal Time

What movements or gestures correspond to the following expressions?

1. Hmm... Je dois réfléchir avant de répondre.

2. Tant pis. Qu'est-ce que ça fait? Ça n'a pas d'importance.

3. Ça ne va pas, non? Vous êtes fou? Vous conduisez mal!

4. Mon œil! Je ne vous crois pas! Ce n'est pas vrai!

5. Je l'ai échappé belle. Ouf!

6. Ah! Bonjour, Suzanne! Quel plaisir de te voir!

7. Bonjour, Madame Laforêt. Comment allez-vous?

8. Mademoiselle! L'addition s'il vous plaît!

9. Est-ce que je pourrais me servir du téléphone?

10. Qu'est-ce que je m'ennuie! C'est la barbe!

Express these emotions with an interjection:

11. la douleur: Vous vous êtes fait mal.

12. la colère: Vous êtes fâché(e).

13. l'incompréhension: Vous voulez qu'on répète.

14. l'admiration: Quelqu'un porte un nouveau chapeau.

15. l'hésitation: Vous cherchez vos mots.

16. l'approbation: Vous avez aimé le concert.

17. la joie: Vous venez de gagner un prix.

18. l'impatience: Vous voulez que quelqu'un s'en aille.

19. le dégoût: Vous venez de boire du jus qui n'était pas frais.

20. la provocation: Vous proposez à un ami de sauter le ruisseau.

2

Manners

If the French Think You're Rude and You Think
They're Rude, Be Polite the French Way

1. To whom can you say *tu*?

2. What would someone say to you to tell you to use the *tu* form?

3. What's the first thing to say when you walk into a French bakery?

4. How do you say hello to a French doctor?

5. How would you say hello to a French police officer?

6. What should you say before asking directions?

7. What does *S'il vous plaît!* mean with an exclamation mark?

8. What is meant by *Je vous en prie*?

9. When do people say *Désolé*?

10. Where would you say *Après vous*?

11. What do French parents say to get their children to say *Merci*?

12. What's the follow-up prompt from parents if the child just says *Merci*?

13. What is meant by *Merci, mon chien*?

14. At what hour of the day do you start saying *Bonsoir*, and what's the difference among *Bonsoir*, *Bonne soirée*, and *Bonne nuit*?

15. How do you say "Have a good vacation"?

16. What should you say to make light of a faux pas?

17. How does the meaning of *Ils sont bien élevés* change when applied to children and when applied to adults?

18. When would you hear someone say *Du tout, du tout*?

19. What is meant by *le quart d'heure français*?

20. What's the literal meaning of *Au revoir*, and why do the French often add expressions like *A bientôt* and *A demain*?

Don't expect your American manners to have the same results in France as they do in the United States. By adopting the more formal French manners, however, you will have a chance to observe French politeness.

The polite words *excusez-moi, s'il vous plaît,* and *merci* are easily recognized as some of the most important words to learn, but often they are thought to be interchangeable with their English counterparts. A key aspect of learning French manners is to know how and when to use the *formules de politesse.* The *formules* are useful both as French expressions and as ways of using nonverbal communication effectively.

Our own manners in our own country are instinctive. Like Molière's Monsieur Jourdain, *le bourgeois gentilhomme* who didn't realize he'd been speaking prose all his life, we don't realize we've been using manners all our lives.

If you're not French, though, you can assume that you haven't been using French manners all your life. "French manners" may even seem like an oxymoron to outsiders, but learning French manners opens the door to understanding French culture and liking the French.

So Who's Ruder?

The French think Americans are rude, and Americans think the French are rude. Americans are said to act too busy to greet people and thought to talk too loudly in restaurants. France is the world's favorite travel destination, but the French are considered condescending and argumentative. The jury is out on who's ruder, but everyone has an opinion. It may be impossible to get an objective answer on this other than that it's just a matter of a different cultural bias.

My observation, though, has always been that overall the French are, at least in France, more considerate than Americans. The French are perhaps ruder in the United States.

The French in general appear to me to be above average in real manners, not just rituals. I've found this true both of strangers and of friends. Strangers in France lend me their cell phones. They not only give directions but help me find my way. French children have, on the whole, had more training in manners, in social rituals, and in respect for others than American children. Social scientists are now discovering a connection between family rituals and health, so there's some scientific evidence for the benefits of the French kind of politeness.

The formality of manners opens the door to making French friends. The trusting exchange of ideas becomes easier, and the exchange of controversial ideas becomes possible when everyone is polite and respectful.

The French often say that they have trouble themselves with the use of *tu* and *vous*. Usually, but not always, they say *tu* to someone with whom they're on a first-name basis. It's actually easier if you're not French because you can just say *vous* to everyone over sixteen until you're told to say *tu*. (*Mais on peut se tutoyer!*)

The use of the term *savoir-vivre* (literally, "to know how to live") to refer to the rules of etiquette and good manners conveys the great importance of good manners to the French. The basis for thinking that the French are rude comes largely from the fact that French businesspeople, salespeople, and waiters have different manners than their American counterparts. The French "smile campaign" of the seventies never completely caught on, but again in 1994 France launched a *bonjour* campaign that was renewed in the summer of 2003 with thousands of posters of happy Parisians and the slogan "Our smile comes from the heart."

French shopkeepers expect you to say *Bonjour, monsieur* and *Bonjour, madame*. They insist on good manners from their customers. The American customer is used to being "always right" and expects good manners from salespeople.

While many French waiters are impressively knowledgeable and helpful, some individual waiters have raised the French variety of rudeness to an art form famous around the world. They have helped to create the stereotype of the snobby French waiter, which in turn has led to a stereotype about the French. In reality, the French tend to be rude to Americans only when their place is overrun by tourists or they are responding to perceived rudeness in others.

In French a verb can be more polite if it's in the right grammatical mood. You can sound more polite just by remembering to use the conditional for politeness. Try adjusting the following two sentences to fit your needs.

Je voudrais un crayon/une aspirine/un thé.
Pourriez-vous fermer la fenêtre/ouvrir la fenêtre/me passer le sucre?

The French magic words can at first seem deceptively easy because they seem to be straightforward equivalents of the magic words in English. In reality, though, it's a lot easier to know the French *formules* than to know how and when to use them.

Bonjour, Madame la Ministre

The French *bonjour* only works magic when you use it differently from the way you'd use "hello." You say *bonjour* individually to each person in a small group of friends. You say *Bonjour, monsieur* or *Bonjour, madame* to a shopkeeper whom you do not call by his or her first name—and with whom you probably will never be on a first-name basis. The school principal is called *Monsieur le Directeur* or *Madame la Directrice*, so you have to be able to say *Bonjour, Madame la Directrice* without feeling stuffy or absurd. Even if you call a friend by his or her first name, you say the first name, almost as a title, along with *bonjour* or *salut*—not always, but more often than in English.

The rules for addressing women are evolving. In 1992 Edith Cresson was called *Madame le Premier Ministre* in France, but in 1993 Kim Campbell was called *la première ministre déléguée* in Canada. In 1997 France followed Canada, Switzerland, and Belgium in giving feminine forms to some professions that had previously had only masculine forms, such as *ministre*.

TOP TEN Rules About *bonjour*

1. On dit «Bonjour, monsieur», «Bonjour, madame», ou «Bonjour, mademoiselle», à quelqu'un qu'on n'appelle pas par son prénom.

2. On peut dire «Salut», à un copain ou à une copine.

3. On dit «Bonjour, madame», à la pâtissière avant d'acheter un croissant.

4. On dit «Bonjour, madame», à une femme même si elle n'est pas mariée.

5. On peut dire «Bonjour, Madame la Ministre», depuis 1997.

6. On dit «Bonjour, Monsieur le Directeur», ou «Bonjour, Madame la Directrice», au directeur ou à la directrice d'une école.

7. On dit «Bonjour, Monsieur l'Agent», ou «Bonjour, Madame l'Agent», à un agent de police avant de lui poser une question.

8. Il faut dire «Bonjour, Docteur», à un docteur ou à un(e) dentiste et «Bonjour, Maître», à un(e) avocat(e) ou un(e) notaire.

9. On ne dit pas «Bonjour», dans la rue à quelqu'un qu'on ne connaît pas.

10. On ne doit pas dire «Bonjour, messieurs dames», mais «Bonjours, messieurs, bonjour, mesdames».

Les formules de politesse

Context is important in determining whether a *formule de politesse* is really polite or not. Consider the various meanings of the following expressions.

Excusez-moi

Excusez-moi obviously means "Excuse me." "I'm sorry for what I did." "I apologize." It can't be said too often. *Excusez-moi* is also a polite and effective way to start a request. You go about asking for directions by saying *Pardon* or *Excusez-moi de vous déranger*. Then you go on with your request: *Pourriez-vous m'indiquer la rue Monsieur le Prince, s'il vous plaît?* "Excuse me for bothering you. Could you give me directions to the rue Monsieur le Prince, please?"

Excusez-moi can also mean "Please let me get by." Excuse me for something I'm about to do anyway, such as squeeze past you to get to my seat at the movies.

Finally, a classic introduction to disagreeing with someone is *Excusez-moi de le dire mais vous vous trompez*. "Pardon me for saying so but you're wrong." In this context, *excusez-moi* is not really polite at all, but fake polite.

S'il vous plaît

Like *excusez-moi*, *s'il vous plaît* is an amazingly versatile expression. *Un café, s'il vous plaît* is just "I'd like coffee, please." But *s'il vous plaît* is said much more often than one says "please" in English. *S'il vous plaît!* is also used to get someone's attention. So *s'il vous plaît! Un café, s'il vous plaît* would be "Waiter! Coffee, please." Saying *s'il vous plaît!* works better than snapping fingers when trying to get the attention of a salesperson or a waiter, but it's the same idea.

S'il vous plaît can also be used as an opener in the same way as *excusez-moi* when asking directions. Again, you can use it twice, once to accost the person and the second time to be polite. *S'il vous plaît! Où se trouve la rue St. Paul, s'il vous plaît?* However, it's more polite and much more productive to start out with *Excusez-moi de vous déranger*, even though it takes more time.

S'il vous plaît can be used in a unique way in addition to the previous meanings. Consider the following sentence: *Et elle descend tou-*

jours au Ritz, s'il vous plaît! "And she always stays at the Ritz, no less." So *s'il vous plaît* can be used in an ironic way to mean "no less" or "if you please" in a sentence about someone who's ostentatious.

Au revoir

Au revoir usually comes with a form of address or a name in the same way as *bonjour* and *merci*. Note that *au revoir* combines *au* and *revoir* to mean "until we see each other again." What makes *au revoir* a polite expression is its literal meaning. In leave-taking, the idea of seeing each other again should usually be made even more explicit by the mention of exactly when the rendezvous will take place. More on that later.

Je vous en prie

Je vous en prie is another classic *formule de politesse* with a flexible meaning: *Je vous en prie* means "please" as in *Après vous, je vous en prie*, "Please, go ahead," and in *Dites oui, je vous en prie*, "Please say yes."

In reply to *Merci*, the French say *Je vous en prie* to mean "You're welcome." But in reponse to *Excusez-moi*, when they say *Je vous en prie* it means "No problem."

Je vous en prie means "Go right ahead" in response to *Vous permettez?* Typically, someone will ask *Vous permettez?* before smoking, and someone else will say *Je vous en prie*.

However, *Je t'en prie* can be said with annoyance as in *Je t'en prie, ça suffit!* "For goodness sake, cut it out!" This is another example of the importance of context in determining whether a *formule de politesse* is really polite or not.

Je suis désolé

Je suis désolé(e) means "I'm sorry." But not "I'm desolate." *Je suis désolé(e) de vous avoir dérangé(e).* "I'm sorry to have bothered you."

Je suis désolé. Je n'ai pas le temps means "Sorry. I don't have time." *Désolé(e)* like *Je regrette* becomes another way of saying no when said by itself.

Vous permettez?

Vous permettez? is very useful as a way of announcing an otherwise aggressive intention in a way that sounds polite: "May I?" "Do you mind?" It can mean just, "Do you mind if I sit here?" But it probably means, "I'm going to sit here," "Do you mind if I smoke?" or "You'll have to move your coat." The typical response is still *Je vous en prie.* "No problem."

Je suis très heureux de faire votre connaissance

Je suis très heureux/heureuse de faire votre connaissance means "It's a pleasure to meet you" or "How do you do." Most people just say *bonjour* when they are introduced, and this is acceptable. The famous *Je suis enchanté(e) de faire votre connaissance* is becoming more unusual. *Très heureux* and *très heureuse* and *enchanté* and *enchantée* are not as welcome as the longer expressions. It's ideal to say *Je suis heureux de faire votre connaissance,* but *bonjour* is preferable to the cursory *très heureux* or *enchanté.*

Après vous

Après vous, "After you," is always a polite thing to say at a doorway. And the correct reply is usually, *Non, après vous.* Who goes first is determined by a certain hierarchy: women before men, older women before younger women, and so forth. But the trick is to act clueless about the hierarchy and just treat the other person as more worthy than you to go through the door first. In some circles you can't go from *le salon* to *la salle à manger* without a few back-and-forths of *Après vous. Non, après vous.* There's a name for this: *la bataille de la porte.* In other circles, people also say *Après vous* as they go through the door to the dining room, but as a joke.

TOP TEN *Formules de politesse,* in Order of Importance

1. **Excusez-moi.**

2. **S'il vous plaît!**

3. **Bonjour...**

4. **Au revoir...**

5. **Merci...**

6. **Je vous en prie...**

7. **Je suis désolé(e)...**

8. **Vous permettez?**

9. **Je suis très heureux de faire votre connaissance.**

10. **Après vous.**

On ne dit pas merci? Merci, qui? Merci, mon chien.

When American children forget to say "thank you," they are prompted with "What do you say?" French children are prompted with, *On ne dit pas merci?* "You don't say thank you?" Then when the French child says *merci*, there's another prompt: *Merci, qui?* "Who are you thanking?" A child who attaches someone's name to *merci, bonjour,* and *au revoir* is *un enfant bien élevé.* Another expression sometimes used to prompt children to add a name or title is *Merci, mon chien,* "Thank you, my dog." Balzac is said to have started this expression. French children are taught that adding names and titles is just as important as the words *merci* and *s'il vous plaît* themselves.

As well as responding with the very polite *Je vous en prie,* "You're welcome" (literally, I pray you), you may respond to *merci* with the rather formal, *C'est la moindre des choses,* "It's really nothing, the smallest of things." More informally you say, *Il n'y a pas de quoi,*

"There is nothing for which to thank me," or *Ce n'est rien* or *De rien*, "It's nothing" or "For nothing."

TOP TEN Ways to Say "Thank You"

1. **Merci, monsieur. Merci, madame.** Thank you, sir. Thank you, ma'am.

2. **Merci, Monsieur le Directeur. Merci, Madame la Directrice.** Thank you, Head of School. (thank you with a title)

3. **Un grand merci.** A big thank-you.

4. **Merci bien.** Thanks.

5. **Merci beaucoup.** Thanks a lot.

6. **Je vous remercie. (Je te remercie.)** I thank you. (a bit more formal, therefore more polite)

7. **Merci mille fois.** Many, many thanks. ("A thousand thank-yous" is not over the top.)

8. **Je vous suis très reconnaissant(e).** I'm very grateful.

9. **Merci infiniment.** Thanks tremendously. (infinitely)

10. **Je suis confus(e).** I don't know how to thank you. I'm overcome, confused.

Bonne journée

The French complain that "Have a nice day" sounds superficial and many Americans agree. But the French say *Bonne journée*, "Have a nice day," constantly, and use *bon* and *bonne* for every major and minor occasion without feeling the slightest bit superficial. In French *bonne journée* is a gracious *formule de politesse*, like *s'il vous plaît* and *merci*, whereas "Have a nice day" comes across as a telemarketer's cliché.

Bonjour is hello and *Bonne journée* is good-bye. Around 6:30 P.M. you switch from *Bonjour* to *Bonsoir*. *Bonsoir* is both hello and good-bye in the evening, but it's different from *Bonne soirée*, which you say when someone is leaving for the evening, perhaps to go to a movie.

The popularity of expressions with *bon* is demonstrated by the expression *Bonne continuation*. You can say *Bonne continuation* on almost any occasion. Waiters will sometimes wish you *Bonne continuation* as they temporarily take leave between the courses of a meal.

The French say *bon* this or that intuitively as one of the ways to end a conversation with finesse. In French you too should sign off with a good wish. It's a way of leaving someone without sounding abrupt, and it forms a transition to whatever's coming up next.

TOP TEN Ways to Sign Off from a Short Conversation

1. **Bonne journée!** Have a good day.

2. **Bon après-midi!** Have a good afternoon.

3. **Bonne fin d'après-midi!** Enjoy the rest (end) of the afternoon.

4. **Bonne soirée!** Have a good evening.

5. **Bonne nuit!** Sleep well. (good night)

6. **Bonne fin de semaine!** Have a good weekend.

7. **Bon week-end!** Have a good weekend.

8. **Bon dimanche!** Enjoy your Sunday.

9. **Bonne santé!** Stay well!

10. **Bonne continuation!** Enjoy the rest of your meal or your trip. Enjoy continuing with whatever you're doing.

Bonne route

The expressions with *bon* and *bonne* are easy to understand but counterintuitive for Americans to use. Fortunately we already say *Bon voyage!* in English. In English we don't say "Have a bon voyage." Make *Bon voyage!* your model for other *bon* and *bonne* expressions to break the habit of bringing the equivalent of a "have a" structure to French. *Bonne route* is enough for "Have a safe trip." You hear *Bonnes vacances!* more often than *Passez de bonnes vacances*.

Bonne fête! literally means "good party" or "good celebration." It could be said at any celebration but may refer in particular to someone's saint's day. France being a largely Catholic country, many people are named after saints and they celebrate the day of the saint by the same name as well as celebrating their own birthdays. It's considered particularly discreet to wish a woman *Bonne fête* on her saint's day rather than *Bon anniversaire* on her birthday. By saying *Bonne fête*, the delicate matter of bringing up a woman's age is avoided.

The much admired expression *Bon courage* has a counterpart in the United States in the increasingly common expression, "Courage." *Bonne* goes with *chance* in the expression *Bonne chance!* "Good luck!" However, *Vous avez de la chance. Vous n'avez pas de chance.* "You have good luck," and "You have bad luck" are literally, "You have luck," and "You don't have luck."

TOP TEN Good Wishes

1. **Bon anniversaire!** Happy birthday!

2. **Bon voyage!** Have a good trip!

3. **Bonne fête!** Enjoy the party!

4. **Bon appétit!** Enjoy your meal!

5. **Bon courage!** Take heart!

6. **Bonne chance!** Good luck!

7. **Bonne route!** Have a safe trip!

8. **Bonnes vacances!** Have a good vacation!

9. **Bonne fin de séjour!** Enjoy the rest of your stay!

10. **Bonne année!** Happy New Year!

Il faut en offrir à tout le monde

If you have something that can be shared, you share with everyone present. To be inclusive is one of the French ways to be polite. In France no one eats, drinks, or smokes in a group without inviting everyone to partake. Cigarettes are offered around, even to a half-a-dozen people. People rarely eat between meals, but if they do have candy occasionally, everyone is invited to have some. For Americans, of course, offering cigarettes around to a group is not thoughtful. On the other hand, Americans who smoke think that the French are thoughtful to leave them alone.

Bien dormi?

To be solicitous is another way to be polite. There's less small talk about sports in France, and somewhat more about the health of the family, *Tout le monde va bien à la maison?* and about whether people slept well. At night: *Bonne nuit, Dormez bien (Dors bien), Faites de beaux rêves (Fais de beaux rêves)*. First thing in the morning: *Bien dormi?*

  Soyez le bienvenu, Soyez la bienvenue is "It's good to see you! Welcome!" *Bienvenue en France!* is "Welcome to France!"

TOP TEN Things to Say to Show You Care About Your Guests

1. **Soyez le bienvenu.** Welcome.

2. **Entrez.** Come in.

3. **Par ici.** Come this way.

4. **Ne vous dérangez pas.** Don't get up. Don't go to any trouble.

5. **Faites comme chez vous.** Make yourself at home.

6. **Attention à la marche.** Watch your step.

7. **Tout le monde va bien à la maison?** Is your family/household well? (in conversation with casual acquaintances)

8. **Vous avez tout ce qu'il vous faut?** Do you have everything you need?

9. **Dormez bien. Faites de beaux rêves.** Sleep well. Sweet dreams.

10. **Bien dormi?** Did you sleep well?

Un faux pas

A *faux pas*, a false step, is a French concept. There's concern for doing things the right way, and there's also a process for smoothing things over if there's a *faux pas*. The French have a lot of different ways of righting a *faux pas*, putting people at ease with soothing expressions. These expressions tend to be in the negative because they are about not worrying.

The first eight of the ten expressions for responding to a *faux pas* are in the negative, and the tenth expression only works for a sneeze. *A vos souhaits!* (*A tes souhaits!*) is the French for "Gesundheit!" (literally, "To your wishes. May your wish come true.")

TOP TEN Agreeable Things to Say to Make Light
of a *faux pas*

1. **Ça ne fait rien.** It's nothing.

2. **Ce n'est pas grave.** It's nothing. (e.g., the stain from something spilled)

3. **Il n'y a pas de mal.** No harm done. (a reply to an apology for something clumsy, something spilled)

4. **Ne vous faites pas de souci. (Ne te fais pas de souci.)** Don't worry about it.

5. **Ne vous en faites pas. (Ne t'en fais pas.)** Don't give it a second thought. Don't worry about it. (*en = de souci*)

6. **Ne vous inquiétez pas. (Ne t'inquiète pas.)** Don't worry.

7. **Pas de problème.** No problem.

8. **N'y pensez plus. (N'y pense plus.)** Don't give it another thought.

9. **C'est normal.** That's understandable.

10. **A vos souhaits! (A tes souhaits!)** Bless you! Gesundheit!

Bien élevé, mal élevé

While George W. Bush was calling three countries "evil," Jacques Chirac was calling other countries *mal élevés*. These leaders created a stir in both countries by the great divides between good and evil, and between *bien élevé* and *mal élevé*.

When applied to a child, *bien élevé* can mean well brought up and well behaved. Since children are *bien élevés* or *mal élevés* according to whether their parents are perceived as having done a good job of raising them, the moral responsibility for someone *mal élevé* rests, until age eighteen or so, with the child's parents.

When *bien élevé* is applied to an adult it means respectful, considerate, ethical, independent, and mature. One of the meanings of *éducation* in French has to do with politeness. Someone who's *bien élevé(e)* is said to have been *éduqué(e)*, educated.

To be *bien élevé* means "to get it," to know what's expected of you, and to take on your social responsibilities. In practice, the closest equivalent to *mal élevé* would be "ignorant." You can speak of people as being *bien élevé* at any age, but after the age of about ten, you don't actually tell someone he or she is *bien élevé(e)*. There are other ways of expressing approval.

TOP TEN Ways to Express Approval

1. **Félicitations. Toutes mes félicitations.** Congratulations.

2. **Je vous félicite. (Je te félicite.)** Congratulations. I congratulate you.

3. **A la bonne heure!** Well done! Very good!

4. **Vous avez l'air en forme. (Tu as l'air en forme.)** You look fit.

5. **Cela nous fait très plaisir.** We're delighted (by your gift, your visit . . .).

6. **Il est bien. Elle est bien.** He/She is a good person.

7. **Il est bien élevé. Elle est bien élevée.** He/She is well behaved. (for adults: respectful, considerate, ethical, independent, and mature)

8. **C'est parfait.** This is just right. (You chose a perfect gift.)

9. **Ça vous va très bien. (Ça te va très bien.)** That looks very good on you.

10. **Vous avez bonne mine. (Tu as bonne mine.)** You look well.

Je vous invite

A polite way to make it clear that you intend to pay at a restaurant is to use the verb *inviter* when you make a plan. *Je vous invite* or *Je t'invite* means both "I invite you" and "I'll pay." You wouldn't use the verb *inviter* in that context if you weren't intending to pay. If someone says *Je vous invite*, you can reply, *C'est très gentil de votre part.*

Certain polite responses are automatic. Even if you are ready for your guests to leave, you are expected to say *Déjà?* when they finally say they're going to leave. And if you are not free to accept an invitation it's polite to suggest *une autre fois* so as not to seem too abrupt. It's good to express reciprocity for good wishes such as *Bonne soirée* by replying, *A vous aussi* or *A toi aussi.*

People do actually say *Vous êtes trop aimable*—too amiable, too nice—when accepting a gift, but it's too formal an expression to be used in a *tu* form.

It's polite to argue a bit with someone who wants to pay the bill: *Il n'en est pas question*, and with someone who wants to reimburse you, *Cela peut attendre.* If someone says *Ça vous dérange?* you may hear the reply *Du tout, du tout*, which comes from *pas du tout.*

TOP TEN   Polite Responses to Invitations and Social Gestures

1. **Vous êtes trop aimable.** You're very kind, too kind.

2. **C'est très gentil de votre/ta part.** That's very nice of you.

3. **Une autre fois.** Another time.

4. **Déjà?** You have to leave already?

5. **A vous aussi. A toi aussi.** You too.

6. **Il n'en est pas question.** I wouldn't dream of letting you.

7. **Cela peut attendre.** That can wait.

8. **Dites-lui bien des choses de ma part.** Give him/her my best.

9. **Volontiers.** With pleasure.

10. **Du tout, du tout.** (*Pas du tout.*) Not at all.

Excusez-moi d'être en retard

L'exactitude est la politesse des rois is a sentence attributed to Louis XVIII, meaning that punctuality is the highest form of courtesy, the king's politeness. On the other hand, for those who aren't kings, it's not considered polite to arrive exactly on time. Ten minutes late is considered ideal in France, and there's a special expression for being fifteen minutes late: *le quart d'heure français*, meaning the traditional fifteen minutes late.

Arriving more than fifteen minutes late is considered rude. If you are more than ten minutes late, it's polite to offer an excuse. If you are more than twenty minutes late, you must. Here are some of the most common ones. Start each excuse with *Excusez-moi d'être en retard* or *Excuse-moi...* or *Je suis désolé(e) d'être en retard*.

The expression, *Je me suis trompé(e) de porte* is useful as a model. As well as *Je me suis trompé(e) d'escalier*, you could also say *Je me suis trompé(e) de rue*, *Je me suis trompé(e) de train, de métro*, and so forth.

TOP TEN   Excuses for Being Late

1. **Je me suis trompé(e) de porte.** I went to the wrong door.

2. **Je me suis trompé(e) d'escalier.** I went up the wrong staircase.

3. **J'ai raté le train.** I missed the train.

4. **J'ai manqué l'autobus.** I missed the bus.

5. **Je ne connaissais pas le chemin.** I didn't know the way.

6. **Je me suis perdu(e).** I got lost.

7. **J'ai dû attendre un taxi.** I had to wait for a taxi.

8. **J'avais un coup de téléphone.** I had a phone call.

9. **Ma montre s'est arrêtée.** My watch stopped.

10. **Il y avait beaucoup de circulation.** There was a lot of traffic.

Au revoir, à demain

The French good-bye, *au revoir*, literally means "until we see each other again." This is telling because the French do, in fact, specify when they will see each other again, even if it's just in a few minutes: *A tout de suite.*

The French are not particularly aware that they do this or that they feel a need for it. It's just a reflex. Still, in order to seem polite and friendly you should point out, using the appropriate formula, that you will see each other again and when that will be.

As informal alternatives to *au revoir* you can say *salut* or *tchao*. *Salut* can be either hi or bye. But *tchao*, the French spelling of *ciao*, is perhaps the most frequent informal good-bye. In slang, it might be just *Allez, je m'tire*, "I'm outta here."

TOP TEN Ways to Tell People When You'll See Them Again

1. **A tout de suite!** I'll be right with you. See you in a sec.

2. **A tout à l'heure!** See you later!

3. **A bientôt!** See you soon!

4. **A cet après-midi.** See you this afternoon.

5. **A demain!** See you tomorrow.

6. **A samedi!** See you Saturday.

7. **A la semaine prochaine!** See you next week!

8. **A lundi en huit!** See you a week from Monday!

9. **A la prochaine!** Till next time! (familiar and discouraged by some who insist on *A la prochaine fois*)

10. **A un de ces jours!** See you one of these days.

Rehearsal Time

Give the expression with *bon* or *bonne*, such as *bon voyage* or *bonne journée*, suggested by the following cues:

1. Amusez-vous bien au théâtre!

2. Dormez bien!

3. J'espère que vous n'allez pas tomber malade.

4. Ne soyez pas découragé!

5. C'est le premier janvier.

How would you say hello in French to the following people?

6. à la boulangère

7. à un agent de police

8. à la directrice d'une école

9. à une ministre

10. à un dentiste

Match the responses in the first column with the expressions in the second column, using the letter or letters of the correct expressions.

11. Vous êtes trop aimable.	a. Je vous invite à venir dîner chez nous demain soir.
12. C'est très gentil de votre part.	b. C'est pour vous. Je vous ai apporté des chocolats.
13. Une autre fois.	c. Ça vous dérange?
14. Déjà?	d. Vous en reprendrez?
15. A vous aussi.	e. Vous viendrez avec nous?
16. Il n'en est pas question.	f. Il faut qu'on s'en aille.
17. Cela peut attendre.	g. Bonne journée!
18. Dites-lui bien des choses de ma part.	h. C'est moi qui vous invite.
19. Volontiers.	i. Je dois vous rembourser.
20. Du tout, du tout. (Pas du tout.)	j. Pierre ne pouvait pas venir mais il vous dit bonjour.

Idioms to Go

Get Extra Mileage from Your French by Using Everyday Idioms That Are Both Easy and Authentic

Preview

1. What does *alors* mean, and what's the difference between saying *Ça alors* and *Alors là*?

2. In French, how can you ask in two words what happened next?

3. When would you say *Forcément*?

4. What does *Doucement!* mean as an order?

5. What's meant by *Effectivement* as a one-word expression?

6. What two-word expression is used the same way as "Coming up!" in restaurants?

7. What's the difference between saying *Je veux* and *Je veux bien*?

8. What's meant by saying *Belote et rebelote*?

9. What two French clichés are associated with primary-school teachers trying to get a class to quiet down?

10. What two-word expressions, meaning literally "So much the better" and "So much the worse," did Laurence Sterne call the two "great hinges of French conversation"?

11. In French how do you say "to make a long story short" in one word?

12. How do you say in French "They can't stop laughing"?

13. What is *une grande surface*?

14. What are all of the possible meanings of *on*?

15. What activities are referred to by *ça* in these expressions: *Plus jamais ça!* and *Il pense toujours à ça*?

16. What two words do you use if you want someone to get out of your way in the subway?

17. How do the French say "Don't forget to write!"

18. How do you say "Does she ever smoke!"

19. What's the French expression for "My! How you've grown!"

20. How would you say "What difference does it make?"

If you need to break the habit of translating literally from English to French, tune up with short idioms. The expressions in this chapter are the basic idioms that draw you into the flow of everyday language. They aren't fancy expressions, and they probably won't help you buy anything or reserve a room—that's in the next chapter—but they will go a long way toward making you feel and sound more French.

This tune-up concerns the importance of learning whole expressions. It provides both one-of-a-kind idioms and some idiomatic structures that can serve as models for other expressions.

Most of the vocabulary words in this section will look familiar, but instead of seeing them in a vocabulary list, you will see them recycled in idioms. In most cases, the meaning of an idiom differs from the meaning of its individual words. For example, the expression *quand même* is composed of the two words *quand* and *même*, which literally mean "when" and "the same." In a sentence *quand même* means "all the same" or "even so." But the exclamation *Quand même!* means "That's going too far!" or "Honestly!"

Using these idioms will build your confidence. A short expression can be just as sophisticated as a long expression and will probably sound better. You can appear more fluent using a two-word expression appropriately than trying to say something overly complicated. Short expressions are used constantly in everyday situations, so it's a good idea to have a basic repertoire of these and to know when to use them. They're simple enough so that you can concentrate on how and when you say them without having to use all of your energy just to remember them.

Alors...

Alors is probably one of the most versatile words in French. Like *oui* and *non*, given with ten variations in the Quick Fixes section, *alors* can have many nuances. But it can also just be a filler. You can say *alors* while pausing to think of what to say next.

Toward the beginning of Eugène Ionesco's play *Rhinocéros*, the characters exclaim *Ça alors!* one after the other as they see a rhinoceros go by in the middle of town in broad daylight.

Alors non! suggests "That's going too far!" or "What do you think I am? Chopped liver?" But *Alors là* means "Well, I really don't have anything to say about that. You've got me stumped."

Et alors? can indicate that you want to know what happened next. Children say *Et alors?* when you break off from reading a children's story. But when said with a snarl during an argument *Et alors?* implies "You want to make something of it?"

TOP TEN Ways to Use *alors*

1. **Ça alors!** I'm really shocked! That's the limit!

2. **Alors là.** (resignation) Well, I really don't know what to say.

3. **Je vous laisse alors.** Well, I'll be going.

4. **Alors, tu viens?** So, are you coming?

5. **Et alors?** (innocently) What happened next?

6. **Et alors?** (sarcastically) So you want to make something of it?

7. **Mais non, alors!** Absolutely not!

8. **Il fait beau alors je vais y aller à pied.** It's nice out so I'm going to walk there.

9. **Il avait alors vingt ans.** He was twenty at the time.

10. **Alors, n'en parlons plus.** In that case, let's let it go.

Attention!

In *Pantagruel*, François Rabelais's comic novel written in 1532, *le frère* Fredon, a monk, gives only monosyllabic answers to all questions. You don't have to go *that* far, but like *le frère* Fredon, you can still go a long way with a repertoire of one-word expressions.

The point of these expressions is that they have special meanings. *Bon* doesn't just mean "good." *Bon* can also signify "So that's that." A word like *bon* can sound convincingly French although it's just one syllable.

If you say *Voilà!* when something goes right and *Effectivement* when you agree with someone's argument, you will sound fluent. And it's crucial to have *Attention!* on the tip of your tongue so you can warn someone if you think there's going to be an accident.

Exact is an easy word, since it's also an English word, but it may not yet be second nature to you to say *Exact* or *C'est exact* to mean "That's right." *Doucement* is an adverb, but you say it in order to mean "Take it easy" if someone is pushing too hard on a glass door. It means "Settle down!" if children are too aggressive and rowdy.

TOP TEN   One-Word Idioms

1. **Bon.** OK. So that's that. (literally, good)

2. **Vite!** Hurry! (literally, fast)

3. **Courage!** Don't give up! (literally, courage)

4. **Voilà!** That's just what I thought. There it is. (literally, see there)

5. **Exact.** That's right. (literally, exact)

6. **Attention!** Watch out! (literally, attention. *Faites attention!* Pay attention!)

7. **Forcément.** That goes without saying. That's the way it's bound to be. (literally, forcedly)

8. **Doucement.** Easy does it. (literally, softly)

9. **Justement!** Exactly. That's what I think. (literally, rightly)

10. **Effectivement.** That's right. That's the way it is. (literally, actually)

Bien sûr

In the movie *Le Divorce*, Roxy, played by Naomi Watts, points out to her sister Isabel, played by Kate Hudson, that the French always say *Bien sûr* when you tell them something. She's referring to the way *bien sûr* can be used as a put-down, and later in the movie there's an example of it. On the surface *bien sûr* can mean "Of course you're right" while the skeptical tone of the speaker gives the underlying meaning of "Yeah, sure." *Forcément* and *pas forcément* can operate somewhat the same way, but as milder put-downs that make other people feel that their ideas are simplistic.

Ça marche means "Great," "That's OK," "Let's go ahead with that." It's also "Coming up!" when used in restaurants.

Au tableau! is how a teacher tells a student to write something on the blackboard. *Au travail!* and its slang equivalent *Au boulot!* mean "Let's get to work!" Similar orders without verbs are: *Au lit!* "Go to bed!"; *A table!* "Dinnertime!"; *A genoux!* "Get on your knees!"; *A la porte!* "Get out!"; *Au feu!* "There's a fire!"; *Au voleur!* "Stop thief!"; and *Aux barricades!* "To the barricades!" The French national anthem, *La Marseillaise*, includes the line «*Aux armes, citoyens!*» calling on citizens to take up weapons. In François Truffaut's movie *Les 400 Coups*, the teacher punishes Antoine Doinel by calling out sharply, «*Au piquet!*» and sending him to the corner.

A moi is an extremely useful expression if you are in a double line in front of a counter or if someone is about to cut in front of you. You assert your rights with *A moi*. You would say *A vous* or *A toi* if it's the other person's turn. These are the terms used for taking turns playing cards as well.

Bon débarras! is the one common expression with *bon* that won't help you tune up your French manners.

TOP TEN Two-Word Idioms

1. **Bien sûr!** Of course! Yeah sure!

2. **Ça marche.** Great! Coming up!

3. **Au travail! Au boulot!** Let's get to work! Get to work!

4. **En effet.** That's right.

5. **Sans rancune!** No hard feelings. (literally, without a grudge)

6. **A moi. A vous. A toi.** It's my turn. It's your turn.

7. **Pas forcément.** Not necessarily.

8. **Quand même!** That's going too far!

9. **Bon débarras!** Good riddance!

10. **Pas possible!** I don't believe it!

Pas de problème

Pas de problème, "No problem!" is said to be the number one international expression. *Ça m'arrangerait* means "That would suit me" or "That would help me out." Conversely, *Ça m'ennuierait* implies that it would be a nuisance. Or it could be that you would be upset. *Ça m'ennuierait de le voir triste.* "I'd be upset to see him unhappy."

Although *je veux* is "I want," *Je veux bien* means "It's all right" or "It's fine with me." In French when you promise to do something you usually say, *C'est promis* (or *Sans faute*) but not *Je promets*. With

Amusez-vous bien you literally amuse yourself well while avoiding a translation of "a good time."

Rebelote is what you say when you play the king of trumps after playing the queen of trumps in the card game *la belote*. *Rebelote* signals a repetition of *belote*, so *Belote et rebelote* means "Here we go again." "Same old thing." *Plus ça change* is the abbreviated version of *Plus ça change, plus c'est la même chose*. "The more things change, the more they stay the same."

Some other expressions abbreviated to three words from longer expressions are *Reste à savoir* and *Raison de plus*. *Reste à savoir* comes from expressions such as *Il reste à savoir si c'est vrai*, "It remains to be seen whether it's true." *Raison de plus*, "All the more reason," comes from *C'est une raison de plus pour le faire*, "That's another reason to do it."

Some four-word expressions are common too. *Ça vaut la peine* means "It's worth the trouble" or "It's worthwhile." The image, *Ça saute aux yeux*, "It's obvious," literally means "It jumps to your eyes."

TOP TEN Three-Word Idioms

1. **Pas de problème.** No problem.

2. **Ça m'arrangerait.** That would help me out. I'd like that.

3. **Ça m'ennuierait.** That would bother me. I'd rather not.

4. **Je veux bien.** It's all right with me.

5. **C'est promis.** I promise.

6. **Amusez-vous bien! (Amuse-toi bien!)** Have a good time!

7. **Belote et rebelote.** It's the same old thing.

8. **Plus ça change.** Things don't really change.

9. **Reste à savoir.** That remains to be seen.

10. **Raison de plus.** All the more reason.

Tant mieux et tant pis

In *A Sentimental Journey Through France and Italy*, published in 1768, Laurence Sterne made a humorously compelling case for *tant pis* and *tant mieux* as the great hinges of French conversation. He added that a traveler "would do well to get them straight before he gets to Paris."

Sterne gives an example of the distinction between *tant mieux* and *tant pis*. A landlord explains the meanings to Sterne, thinking he was "young at French":

> Tant mieux, toujours, monsieur, *said he, when there is anything to be got*—tant pis, *when there is nothing.*

A number of French expressions embody the kind of dichotomy suggested by *tant mieux* and *tant pis*. Here are, along with *tant mieux* and *tant pis*, some suggestions for consideration as other great hinges of the French language.

TOP TEN Pairs of Conversational Hinges

1. Acquiescence
   Tant mieux. Good. (Literally, so much the better.)
   Tant pis. So what? (Literally, so much the worse.)

2. Personality
   Il a bon caractère. He's good-natured. (Literally, he has a good personality.)
   Il a mauvais caractère. He's bad-tempered. (Literally, he has a bad personality.)

3. Timing
   Ça tombe bien. Good timing! (Literally, that falls well.)
   Ça tombe mal. Bad timing! (Literally, that falls badly.)

4. Temperament
   Elle est facile à vivre. She's easy to get along with. (literally, easy to live)

Elle est difficile à vivre. She's hard to get along with. (literally, hard to live)

5. Appearance
   Vous avez bonne mine. You look well. (Literally, have a good expression.)
   Vous avez mauvaise mine. You don't look well. (Literally, have a bad expression.)

6. Mood
   Je suis de bonne humeur. I'm in a good mood. (literally, in good humor)
   Je suis de mauvaise humeur. I'm in a bad mood. (literally, in bad humor)

7. Judgment
   Vous avez raison. You're right. (literally, have reason)
   Vous avez tort. You're wrong. (literally, have wrong)

8. Coming and going
   J'arrive. Wait for me. I'm coming.
   Je m'en vais. I'm taking off.

9. Correctness
   C'est vrai. It's true.
   C'est faux. It's false.

10. Clarification
    Ah bon? Is that so?
    Ah bon. So that's that.

Fillers

The word *bref* provides a lot of mileage, meaning "to make a long story short." If *tant pis* and *tant mieux* are the hinges of conversation, then short expressions like *bref*, *au fond*, and *en gros* are the grease that keeps a French conversation moving. They slip into a conversation unnoticed. They're fillers, but it would be hard to converse in French without them. They are the short expressions that, properly inserted, make you sound as though you can improvise in French.

TOP TEN Fillers

1. **Au fond.** Really. *Je n'ai pas vraiment besoin de carottes au fond.* I really don't need carrots after all.

2. **En gros.** Roughly. *Je peux vous le dire en gros.* I can give you a general idea.

3. **C'est que.** It's just that. *C'est que je n'ai pas vraiment eu le temps.* It's just that I didn't really have time.

4. **A mon avis.** In my opinion. *A mon avis, ils ont tort.* In my opinion they're wrong.

5. **Dans l'ensemble.** On the whole. *Dans l'ensemble, ce n'est pas une mauvaise idée.* On the whole it's not a bad idea.

6. **Si tu veux.** If you like. *On s'est disputé un peu, si tu veux, mais c'est tout.* We had a little quarrel, if you want to call it that, but that's all.

7. **A propos.** By the way. *A propos tu viens ce soir?* By the way, are you coming tonight?

8. **Bref. (Enfin bref.)** To make a long story short. *Bref nous avons décidé de partir.* To make a long story short, we decided to leave.

9. **Mais vraiment.** But after all, that's going too far. *Mais vraiment, c'est trop fort.* Give me a break.

10. **En tout cas.** In any case. *Ils sont là en tout cas.* In any case, there they are.

Ils ont beau travailler, ils ne vont pas réussir

In this top ten list, familiar adjectives create unexpected meanings in the context of whole expressions. This often happens with *grand* as in *un grand film*, "a feature film"; *les grandes lignes*, "the major train lines"; and *la grande route*, "the highway." *Un grand magasin* is a department store. *Les grandes surfaces* are the *hypermarchés*, the giant all-purpose supermarkets like *Carrefour* that have sprung up in malls.

Une grande école is a very competitive institution of higher learning. For engineering, there's *l'Ecole polytechnique*; for leadership in politics, there's *l'Ecole nationale d'administration*; and for teachers, there's *l'Ecole normale supérieure*. These *grandes écoles* all have competitive examinations for entrance, and students are paid by the government during the time they are enrolled.

One of the most unusual uses of an adjective is the use of *beau* in an expression such as *Ils ont beau travailler, ils ne vont pas réussir*. "It's no use for them to work, they won't succeed." *Ils ont beau…* will always mean "They're doing something in vain." As for *belle*: *Ils l'ont échappé belle* means "They had a close call."

TOP TEN Unpredictable Adjectives

1. **Nous avons fait la *grasse* matinée.** We slept in. (literally, greasy morning)

2. **La note est *salée*.** The bill is steep, too high. (literally, salted bill)

3. **C'est mon *petit* ami.** That's my boyfriend. (literally, little)

4. **Nous avons le cœur *gros*.** We have a heavy heart. (literally, fat heart)

5. **Carrefour est une *grande* surface.** Carrefour is a giant all-purpose supermarket. (literally, big surface)

6. **Je vais demander à une *bonne* sœur.** I'll ask a nun. (literally, good sister)

7. **Je suis en *pleine* forme.** I'm in good shape. (literally, full form)

8. **C'était un mariage *blanc*.** It was an unconsummated marriage. (literally, white)

9. **Ils ont le *fou* rire.** They can't stop laughing. They've got the giggles. (literally, crazy laugh)

10. **Ils ont *beau* travailler, ils ne vont pas réussir.** It's no use for them to work, they won't succeed.

On dirait

On is used constantly in informal conversation. *On* can be used just to mean "one," as in *On fait ce qu'on peut.* "One does what one can." Most of the time, *on* means "we." *On a largement le temps* can have several possible meanings, however: "I have plenty of time," "You have plenty of time," "He or she has plenty of time," "One has plenty of time," "We have plenty of time," "They have plenty of time," or "There's plenty of time." Instead of needing a different form for each person you can just use *on* for anyone.

The French expression *On est un con* is pronounced without the usual *liaison* between *on* and *est*. Without the *liaison*, the sentence means that using the word *on* is idiotic. *On est un con* is said in response to someone who starts a sentence with *On dit que...* as a way of passing on received opinions and superstitions.

Les on-dit are the things that people say, the gossip that's passed on without knowing who said it or where it came from. *Le qu'en-dira-t-on* is the concern for appearances.

The following expressions are not of the *on est un con* variety. They can, however, be called *idiotismes* because *un idiotisme* is an idiom.

TOP TEN *Idiotismes* with *on*

1. **Ici on parle français.** French spoken here.

2. **On est jeudi.** It's Thursday.

3. **On dirait.** That's how it seems.

4. **On ne répond pas.** There's no answer.

5. **On vous demande au téléphone.** You're wanted on the phone.

6. **On peut y aller à pied.** It's within walking distance.

7. **On ne sait jamais.** You never know.

8. **On a largement le temps.** There's plenty of time.

9. **On est six.** There are six of us.

10. **On devrait savoir à l'heure qu'il est.** We should know by now.

Ah, ça encore!

Ça is another shortcut, a contraction of *cela*. You rarely hear *cela* in informal conversation, but *ça* is used constantly. When people start talking fast, questions are frequently shortened with *ça*:

Qui ça?	Who's that?
Où ça?	Where was that?
Quand ça?	When was that?
Pourquoi ça?	Why was that?
Comment ça?	How did that happen? What do you mean by that?

Among the idioms with *ça* are: *Pas de ça!* "I'll have none of that!" *On va arroser ça!* "Let's drink to that!" *Ça y est.* "It's finished. All done." And *Ça sent bon.* "Smells good."

Il pense toujours à ça and the variation, *Il ne pense qu'à ça*, usually mean "He only thinks about sex." This could presumably be said in the *elle* form too, but I've never heard it.

Plus jamais ça! is an antiwar slogan since *ça* can connote "war" as well as "sex." "No more war." Since you can have double negatives in French, it's literally: "No longer never that!"

TOP TEN Ways to Use *ça*

1. **Ça va?** How's it going?

2. **Où ça?** Where's that?

3. **Ça ne marche pas.** It's not working.

4. **Ça dépasse tout.** That's the limit.

5. **Ça donne à réfléchir.** That makes you stop and think it over.

6. **Ça m'est égal.** I don't care. (Literally, It's equal to me.)

7. **Ça m'arrive souvent.** That often happens to me.

8. **Ça ne me dit rien.** That doesn't ring a bell.

9. **Ça n'empêche pas.** That doesn't change anything. All the same.

10. **Il pense toujours à ça.** He's always thinking about sex.

Je plaisante

Je plaisante means "I'm just kidding" and *Vous plaisantez* means "You must be joking!" Some of the most interesting French idioms are composed only of a pronoun and verb in the present tense. No direct object. No conjunction. That's it. Suggestive and ripe with possibilities, the sentence is at its most idiomatic when it's at its most simple. The placating cry of someone who's a bit late, *J'arrive!* has already made its way into a top ten list.

Zola's *J'accuse...* at the beginning of a sentence means "I accuse . . . (lots of people . . .)" Standing alone, *J'accuse* means "I'm making an accusation." At the siege of Sebastopol, Marshal MacMahon said, «*J'y suis. J'y reste.*» "I'm here and I'm staying." If you are about to contradict someone, it's customary to start out by saying, *Je regrette—* "I hate to have to disagree."

Je crois, *Je sais*, and *Je comprends* can stand alone as whole utterances and mean "I think so," "I know," and "I understand." *Je crois* can actually mean both "I think so" and "I believe in God." But as a stand-alone idiom it can't mean either "I am thinking" or "I am believing."

The following subject and verb combinations have special meanings as whole expressions in particular situations.

Je réfléchis can mean both "I'm thinking it over" and "I think things over." In a store, *Je réfléchis* gives the message "I'd like to think about it." Say *Je regarde* in a store to mean "I'm just looking."

J'écoute is what you say when you're on the telephone and want the other party to know you're listening. *Vous m'écoutez* without a question mark could mean just "Ah, you're listening to me." But it probably would be said with a sharp tone to mean "You'd better listen to me or else."

Je descends can mean "I'll be downstairs in a moment," but on a train, subway, or a bus it means "I'm getting off."

The comedienne Madeleine Kahn parodied the kind of American teacher who keeps saying to her boisterous class, "I'm waiting . . . I'm waiting." Some French teachers use that line too, only in French they say *J'attends*. Another expression that some teachers like to use is *Un peu de silence!* (with an understated *un peu*) when they are frustrated with the noise level in their classrooms.

You don't need to know complex French sentences to sound as though you know your way around in French. These examples show how much can be implied with a simple subject and verb.

TOP TEN Special Meanings for a Subject and Verb in the Present

1. **Je réfléchis.** I'd like to think about it. (in a store)

2. **Je regarde.** I'm just looking. (in a store)

3. **J'écoute.** Go ahead. (on the phone)

4. **Je descends.** I'm getting off here. (on the bus or subway)

5. **Je regrette.** I'm sorry to have to contradict you. (in the context of starting an argument)

6. **J'attends.** I'm waiting. (in a grade school classroom)

7. **Je plaisante.** I'm just kidding. (when someone's offended)

8. **J'hésite.** I'm hesitating. (in the context of a decision)

9. **J'arrête.** OK. I'm going to cut it out now. (in the context of teasing)

10. **Je rentre.** I'm going home.

Tu ouvres?

In casual conversation, any statement can become a question if your voice goes up at the end. Meaning depends on intonation and punctuation. In François Ozon's movie *Sous le sable* (*Under the Sand*), a husband asks his wife to open the door for him by simply saying *Tu ouvres?* meaning "Can you get the door?" She then opens it for him. If the key had been stuck in the lock he would have said *Tu essaies?* "Could you give it a try?"

With children or other family members, *Tu m'écoutes?* may not be a real question. It usually means, "Listen to me!" during a scolding. And *Tu as compris?* is the sort of thing a stern mother says to her child after delivering an ultimatum. It's not a real question. It's like saying "And I mean it!" Similarly, *Tu as fini?* can mean "Have you finished?" meaning "Have you finished your homework?" If the child is fooling around it means "Stop acting up!"

Vous descendez? (like *Je descends*) is said in the subway. As a question, it's the situational equivalent of "Out please." In France, instead of telling someone on the subway that you want to get off, you ask the person who is in your way if he or she is getting off, even though you may know perfectly well that the person is just blocking your way and has no intention of getting off. So *Vous descendez?* is really a polite way of telling strangers on the subway to get out of your way.

Vous trouvez? is a gracious way of responding to a compliment. In French if you get a compliment on your hat you are not supposed to say "Oh this old thing? It was really cheap," because that would reflect badly on the taste of the person who admired it. And you don't want to sound too conceited either, so you say *Vous trouvez?* acknowledging the compliment and showing a respect for the other person's opinion. Sometimes though, *Vous trouvez?* acknowledges someone's opinion, with a hint of surprise or irony.

Je regarde? is a way of saying to a friend who has an interesting looking photo album, "Do you mind if I look at this?" or "I'd like to take a look."

For *Vous en reprendrez?* the scene is the family dinner table. Again, this is not a real question. It's the way to offer a second helping: "Have some more!"

Vous m'écrirez? is what French people call out at the station at the last minute just as the train is leaving. It doesn't really mean "Will you write to me?" It's a request and a prompt, the equivalent of "Don't forget to write!"

You can say, *Vous permettez?* both when you're offering to help someone lift a suitcase, for example, and when you are taking a liberty, such as smoking in the adjoining seat.

TOP TEN Short Questions That Can Have Two
Different Meanings

1. **Tu ouvres?** Are you opening the door? Open the door.

2. **Tu essaies?** Could you give it a try? I don't think you're really trying.

3. **Tu m'écoutes?** Are you listening to me? Listen to me!

4. **Tu as compris?** Did you understand? And that had better be clear!

5. **Tu as fini?** Have you finished? Stop acting up!

6. **Vous descendez?** Are you getting off? Out please.

7. **Vous trouvez?** Can you find it? I'm glad you like it.

8. **Vous en reprendrez?** Would you like some more? Have some more.

9. **Vous m'écrirez?** Will you write to me? Don't forget to write.

10. **Vous permettez?** Do you allow that? Allow me!

Extra Mileage from Intonation

We've seen that in conversational French, the most frequent kind of question is just formed by changing a period to a question mark. *Vous comprenez?* "You get it?" It can work the other way too. Your voice can also make questions into statements and exclamations. *Qu'est-ce qu'il fume?* is "What's he smoking?" But *Qu'est-ce qu'il fume!* means "Boy, does he ever smoke a lot!"

Similarly, you hear expressions such as *Qu'est-ce qu'elle boit!* "Does she ever drink a lot!" *Qu'est-ce qu'il mange!* "Does he ever eat a lot!" and *Qu'est-ce qu'elle est paresseuse!* "She's really lazy!"

With *Qu'est-ce qu'il boit?* you might be asking innocently enough what he's drinking. Is it water or orange juice? But *Qu'est-ce qu'il boit!* as an exclamation means unmistakably that you can't believe how much he drinks, and you don't mean water.

On a more upbeat note, a non-question that starts like a question could be *Quelle belle journée!* "What a lovely day!" or *Quelle bonne idée!* "What a good idea!"

The first five of the following ten expressions are questions that have come from statements; the second five are exclamations that have come from questions.

TOP TEN   Expressions Created by Intonation

1. **Ça ne te dit rien?** Doesn't that tempt you?

2. **Tu ne viens pas?** Why don't you come?

3. **Tu ne réponds pas?** Answer me.

4. **Tu n'as pas envie d'y aller?** Wouldn't you like to go there?

5. **Elle n'a pas compris?** Didn't she get it?

6. **Qu'est-ce qu'elle fume!** Does she ever smoke!

7. **Qu'est-ce qu'il est paresseux!** Is he ever lazy!

8. **Qu'est-ce que tu as grandi!** My! How you've grown!

9. **Qu'est-ce que tu veux!** What do you expect!

10. **Qu'est-ce que ça peut faire!** It doesn't make any difference.

Rehearsal Time

Say almost the same thing with a one-word expression. Example: *Allez. Il faut vous dépêcher pour être prêt à partir dans dix minutes!* = *Vite!*

1. Fais attention à ce que tu fais!

2. Ne sois pas découragé.

3. Vous devez vous calmer parce que vous faites trop de bruit, les enfants, et vos jeux sont trop aggressifs.

Say the same thing with *on*. Example: *Il n'y a pas de réponse = On ne répond pas.*

4. Nous pouvons y aller en voiture.

5. Je fais ce que je peux.

6. C'est mardi.

7. Ici les gens parlent français.

Convey the same idea in two words. Example: *Je n'arrive pas à me décider. = J'hésite.*

8. C'est mon arrêt. Est ce que je peux passer?

9. Je suis à l'appareil et je vous écoute.

10. Je ne suis pas d'accord avec vous.

11. Attendez-moi, je serai prête dans deux minutes.

12. Je ne sais pas encore si je vais l'acheter ou non mais je vais y réfléchir avant de prendre une décision.

What's the opposite?

13. Tant pis.

14. Il a bon caractère.

15. Ça tombe mal.

16. Vous avez mauvaise mine.

17. Vous avez raison.

18. Ça m'arrange.

19. J'arrive.

20. Elle est facile à vivre.

Practical French

Master the Key Phrases That Go with Specific Situations

Preview

1. In a public place, how do you ask in French where the bathroom is?

2. How do you tell a French salesperson that your purchase is going to be a gift and ask him to gift wrap it for you?

3. How do you say in French "A round-trip ticket, please"?

4. At a gas station, how do you say "Fill it up, please"?

5. When giving directions, what's the difference between *tout droit* and *à droite*?

6. What are the purposes of *un feu orange* and *une carte orange*?

7. What's the difference between *une carte bleue* and *une carte verte*?

8. What can you say to make sure you get a quiet room in a hotel?

9. On the *métro* is there a difference between *un ticket* and *un billet*?

10. What do you say to ask for a book of subway tickets?

11. When speaking of maps, what's the difference between *une carte* and *un plan*?

12. What expression do French salespeople usually use to ask you what you want?

13. In a store, what is meant by *C'est une affaire*, and what's the difference between *une affaire* and *une promotion*?

14. What do French people say when they ask you if you have the right change?

15. What do you say to get the attention of a salesperson in a store?

16. At the market, what's the shorter form of *Combien est-ce que je vous dois?*

17. If you wanted to buy a little more than two pounds of potatoes at the market, how would you ask for that in French?

18. On the telephone, how do you say "Just a moment please"?

19. What's answering-machine French for "Leave a message after the beep"?

20. What kind of computer keyboard do the French use?

This tune-up shows how the French go about daily life. You learn key phrases that help you continue to use French to figure out how the French think. The stock expressions that the French constantly use in particular situations—what the French actually say—is almost always different from what one might guess. There are lots of technically correct French sentences that a French person would not actually use.

When French salespeople ask if your purchase will be a gift, they say, *C'est pour offrir?* rather than *Est-ce que c'est un cadeau?* (still technically correct). So *C'est pour offrir* is what you should say when explaining that a purchase is going to be a gift. The salesperson's next question is *Je vous fais un paquet-cadeau?* "Would you like it gift-wrapped?" (Literally, "I make a package-gift for you?") This is another example of an expression that you would never hit upon from studying French grammar or from translating literally from English to French.

Unless you travel in *la France profonde*, the France without tourists, you will find that people who work in hotels and other tourist locations understand basic English. After all, they needed English to get the job, and they want to show off what they know. Don't take it personally if you're answered in English when you ask a question in French. I saw this happen to a Frenchwoman visiting the site of Cézanne's studio in Aix-en-Provence. When the cashier answered her in English she exclaimed, «*Mais monsieur, je suis française!*» to which he responded, «*Ah, madame, vous savez...* » as if to say, "You know how it is . . . how should I know?"

To shop in France you need not only the right expressions but also their contexts. For example, the French *pharmacie* is an antiseptic and soothing oasis in the middle of town, looking and smelling like something between an American pharmacy counter and a day spa. The pharmacist can give expert advice and recommendations on a variety of ailments. As the American drugstore does not correspond to the concept of a French pharmacy, the French developed *le drugstore*, a hip and shining establishment very different in tone from the American drugstore. The differences were so great that the French version of the American drugstore went back to the United States as *le drugstore*. When the American drive-in movie theater went to France, the French brought champagne to the car windows.

La fromagerie, "cheese shop"; *la charcuterie*, "delicatessen"; *la boulangerie*, "bread shop"; *la poissonnerie*, "fish store"; *la pâtisserie*, "pastry shop"; *la confiserie*, "candy store"; *la diététique*, "health food store"; *la quincaillerie*, "hardware store"; *la papeterie*, "paper store"; and *le bureau de tabac*, which sells tobacco products, stamps, and newspapers are all examples of French shops that need to be experienced to be understood—but not at lunchtime. Between 12 and 3 the sign on the door will probably say *Fermé*.

On January 1, 2002, the French started to use the euro as currency instead of the franc.

En voiture!

At the train station, *En voiture!* means "All aboard!" When you buy a train ticket, it's a good idea to have your requests and questions ready since people are lined up behind you. Most of the time it's enough to know the name of the place where you want to go and to know how to give the essential information: for example, whether you want *un aller-simple*, otherwise known as *un billet simple*, a one-way ticket; or *un aller-retour*, a round trip. The verb *retourner* sometimes causes confusion because it doesn't mean to return to the starting point, as one would expect from *aller-retour*, but rather to go to the same destination again. To discuss *le retour*, saying "I'm returning (here) on Monday," you would have to say *Je reviens lundi*. *Je retourne à Paris* means "I'm going back to Paris for another visit." You can travel *en première classe* or *en deuxième*, which is known as *seconde*.

L'omnibus makes many stops. *L'express* is faster but not as fast as *le TGV*. Reservations are required for *le TGV*, which entails an extra charge. If you forget to validate your ticket for any train, you will have to pay a steep fine. To make sure that you are standing in the right place to get the train to Avignon, you could ask someone, *C'est le bon quai pour Avignon? Le bon quai* is "the right track."

TOP TEN Expressions for Taking the Train

1. **Je voudrais un aller-retour pour Paris pour cet après-midi, s'il vous plaît.** I'd like a round-trip ticket for Paris for this afternoon, please.

2. **En seconde, non-fumeurs, s'il vous plaît.** In second class, no smoking section, please.

3. **Je voudrais réserver deux places dans le TGV pour Avignon, s'il vous plaît.** I'd like to reserve two seats in the TGV for Avignon, please.

4. **Il y a un supplément?** Is there an additional charge?

5. **Le prochain train part à quelle heure?** What time does the next train leave?

6. **Où est-ce que je dois changer?** Where do I have to change?

7. **Combien de temps a-t-on pour prendre la correspondance?** How much time is there to catch the connecting train?

8. **Il y a un wagon-restaurant?** Is there a restaurant car?

9. **C'est à quel quai?** Which track is it on?

10. **Où est-ce que je dois composter le billet?** Where do I validate the ticket?

Le plein

The sign *Location de voitures* is sometimes thought to be about locating cars rather than renting them. *Une voiture de location* is a rented car, just as *une voiture de sport* is a sports car, *une voiture de police* is a police car, and *une voiture de pompiers* is a fire engine. When you get to a gas station, you can say *Le plein, s'il vous plaît* for "Fill it up, please."

A dedicated verb goes with a designated aspect of renting and driving a car. *On* **verse** *les arrhes* (with *arrhes* pronounced like "are" but with the French *r*). *On* **loue** *la voiture, on* **conduit** *la voiture et on* **rend** *la voiture.* Meanwhile, *On* **fait** *le plein, on* **vérifie** *l'huile* and perhaps *la voiture* **tombe** *en panne. Les freins ne* **marchent** *pas, les pneus* **crèvent**. But usually, *Ça marche comme sur des roulettes,* "Everything goes smoothly."

TOP TEN   Expressions for Driving a Car in France

1. **Nous voudrions louer une voiture pour quinze jours.** We'd like to rent a car for two weeks.

2. **C'est combien par semaine?** How much is it per week?

3. **Combien d'arrhes faut-il verser?** What's the deposit?

4. **Où faut-il rendre la voiture?** Where should the car be returned?

5. **On la rend avec le plein?** Do we bring it back with a full tank?

6. **Le plein, s'il vous plaît.** Fill it up, please.

7. **Pourriez-vous vérifier l'huile?** Could you check the oil?

8. **Ma voiture est tombée en panne. (Ma voiture est en panne.)** My car isn't working.

9. **Les freins ne marchent pas.** The brakes don't work.

10. **J'ai un pneu crevé.** I have a flat tire.

Tout droit

When someone gives you directions and says to go *tout droit* you go straight ahead, not *à droite*, "to the right." Traffic lights are *les feux* or *le feu rouge*. *Vous tournez au prochain feu rouge* means "you turn at the next traffic light," which may not actually be red at the time. Otherwise, *Vous avez brûlé un feu rouge*, "You went through a red light" (literally, "You burned a red fire"). *Le feu vert* is the green light, but *le feu orange* is the yellow light.

It's hard to estimate speeds and visualize distances that are expressed with different measurements than you are used to. Your speedometer will register 100 when you're driving under 65 miles an hour. A meter is 39.37 inches and a kilometer is 0.62137 of a mile.

The French don't talk about something being a block or two away but rather would say *C'est à cent mètres* or *C'est à deux cents mètres*. There's a word for a block, *un pâté de maisons*, but it's not used to measure distances.

When getting directions it helps, of course, to have a map. Then you can say *Pourriez-vous me le montrer sur la carte?* If you have a piece of paper, you can ask for a drawing: *Pourriez-vous me faire un dessin?*

If someone asks you for directions and you don't know the answer, you can say *Je ne suis pas d'ici*, "I'm not from around here," or *Je ne peux pas vous dire exactement*, a euphemism for *Je ne sais pas*.

TOP TEN Directions to Give

1. **Vous allez tout droit.** You go straight.

2. **Vous prenez la première rue à droite.** Take the first road on the right.

3. **Vous tournez à gauche.** Turn left.

4. **Vous allez jusqu'au carrefour.** Go as far as the intersection.

5. **C'est un peu plus loin sur la gauche.** It's a little farther on the left.

6. **Vous continuez jusqu'aux feux.** Continue to the traffic light.

7. **Après le feu rouge, vous pouvez rejoindre l'autoroute.**
After the lights, you can get back on the highway.

8. **Vous continuez cent mètres.** Continue about a block (in town). Go about a hundred yards.

9. **Vous allez tomber dessus.** You'll run right into it.

10. **C'est en face.** It's across the street.

Une chambre qui donne sur la cour, s'il vous plaît

Since a room is *une pièce* and a bedroom is *une chambre*, at a hotel you literally ask for a bedroom. *Une chambre pour une personne* or *une chambre individuelle* is a single and *une chambre pour deux personnes* is a double. A double bed is *un grand lit* and *un lit d'appoint* is an extra bed. A hotel that doesn't have vacancies is full, complete, and you will see a sign: *Complet.* Sometimes the price of a room is different according to whether you have it *avec salle de bains*, "with a bathroom with a bathtub," or *avec douche*, "with a shower." In either case there will probably be a separate partition for *les W-C.*

Sometimes the price of breakfast is included in the price of the room. You will be told if it is. You'll sleep better if you remember to ask for *une chambre tranquille* or *une chambre qui donne sur la cour.* *Qui donne sur la cour* means literally, "that gives out onto the courtyard."

TOP TEN Phrases of Hotel French

1. **Vous avez une chambre?** Do you have a vacancy?

2. **C'est pour ce soir.** For tonight.

3. **Je voudrais une chambre avec deux lits et avec salle de bains.** I'd like a room with twin beds and a bathroom.

4. **Je voudrais une chambre avec un grand lit et avec un lit d'appoint si possible, et avec douche, s'il vous plaît.** A room with a double bed and an extra bed if possible, and with a shower, please.

5. **On voudrait une chambre tranquille qui donne sur la cour.** We'd like a quiet room on the courtyard.

6. **On va rester deux nuits.** We'll be staying two nights.

7. **Le petit déjeuner est compris?** Is the price of breakfast included?

8. **Il y a un parking?** Is there a garage?

9. **Je regrette. Je dois annuler pour ce soir.** I'm sorry. I have to cancel for tonight.

10. **Vous êtes complet?** You're full?

C'est combien, un ticket de métro?

The subway, the bus, and the taxi provide cultural fluency as well as transport speed. In a famous interview a reporter once asked Valéry Giscard d'Estaing, then a candidate for president, *C'est combien, un ticket de métro?* "How much is a subway ticket?" to show that Giscard d'Estaing was out of touch with everyday France.

In *le métro, un ticket* is a synonym for *un billet.* Within Paris, the same *ticket* or *billet* can be used for the bus, the subway, and the *RER, Réseau express régional,* an extension of the subway train system. Outside of Paris, a train ticket is always *un billet. Je descends* and *Vous descendez?,* terms from Tune-Up 3, are essential for not missing your stop. You can't transfer to another bus without buying another ticket, though, so it may be worthwhile buying a ticket for unlimited travel—*une carte orange. (Une carte bleue* is a credit card and *une carte verte* is a green card. *Un numéro vert* is a toll-free "800" number.) While a road map is *une carte,* a subway map, like a city map, is *un plan.*

TOP TEN Terms for Getting Around Town

1. **Je voudrais un plan du métro, s'il vous plaît.** I'd like a subway map, please.

2. **Un carnet, s'il vous plaît.** A book of ten tickets, please.

3. **Une carte orange, s'il vous plaît.** A weekly tourist pass, please.

4. **C'est quelle ligne pour aller à la Sorbonne, s'il vous plaît?** What line goes to the Sorbonne, please? (Subway and bus lines go by number.)

5. **C'est quelle direction?** Which direction is it? (The final stop on either end of the line usually indicates the "direction.")

6. **C'est le prochain arrêt.** It's the next stop.

7. **C'est là où on descend.** That's where we get off.

8. **Combien ça va coûter pour aller à Orly?** How much will it cost to go to the Orly airport?

9. **C'est indiqué sur le compteur.** It's marked on the meter. (taxi)

10. **Gardez la monnaie.** Keep the change. (Leave a 10–15 percent tip for the taxi driver.)

Et avec ça?

The most common sales bromides are *Vous désirez? Et avec ça?* and *C'est tout?* The occasional *Je peux vous aider?* can be a way of encouraging you to buy something or get moving.

In the movie *L'Homme du train*, Jean Rochefort tells Johnny Hallyday that he stopped going to a certain bakery because he got angry at *la boulangère* because she always asked *Et avec ça?* with the same singsong tone even though he always bought just one baguette.

Sometimes the standard greetings as people go in and out of shops sound as though they are being sung. In *Les Parapluies de Cherbourg*, an earlier movie by Jacques Demy that was set in an umbrella shop, the characters actually sang lines like *Bonjour, madame* and *Vous désirez?*

When you pay, you may be asked if you wish to use *la carte bleue*, which is a particular kind of credit card that has become a generic term for any credit card. This can lead to confusion. Sometimes only the specific *carte bleue* credit card is accepted at a store or gas station, and sometimes someone will ask for your *carte bleue*, meaning any credit card.

TOP TEN Sales Expressions

1. **Vous désirez?** May I help you?

2. **Et avec ça?** Can I help you with something else?

3. **C'est une affaire.** It's a good deal. (**C'est en solde.** It's on sale.)

4. **Ça vous va très bien.** It looks very good on you.

5. **C'est une promotion.** It's a special.

6. **C'est tout?** Will that be all?

7. **Vous payez à la caisse.** Pay at the register.

8. **A qui le tour?** Who's next?

9. **Comptant ou carte bleue?** Cash or credit?

10. **Vous n'auriez pas la monnaie?** Do you have the right change?

Ce n'est pas ce que je cherchais

Some questions are more often asked in the negative form in French, such as *Vous n'auriez pas la monnaie?* "Do you have the right change?" (literally, "You wouldn't have change?") in the previous top ten list. Another is *Vous n'auriez pas un autre modèle?* "Would you have another style?" (literally, "You wouldn't have another style?") in the following list.

S'il vous plaît! is what you say when you want to draw the salesperson's attention to you, whereas *Je regarde* is what you say when you would prefer to have less attention from a salesperson. You ask for the bathroom by saying, *Où sont les toilettes, s'il vous plaît?*

Ma taille is "my size" for clothes. A child's size is measured by height in *centimètres*, so a one-month size would be 46–56 cm, and 12 months, 76 cm. A boy's or girl's size medium or size 10 would be 140–145 cm. A woman's U.S. dress size 12 is about a 42 in France. A man's shirt size 16 is a 40 in France.

To ask for a bigger size you can say *Vous l'avez en plus grand?* or *Auriez-vous la taille au-dessus?* For a smaller size: *Vous l'avez en plus petit? Auriez-vous la taille au-dessous?*

Ma pointure is "my shoe size." A woman's size 8 shoe is a 39, and a man's size 10 is a 44. It's best not to rely on size, however, since even with a chart of size correspondences you can go wrong. See if the shoe fits, and for clothing ask *Où est le salon d'essayage, s'il vous plaît?* "Where's the dressing room, please?"

TOP TEN Things for You to Say in Stores

1. **S'il vous plaît!** Excuse me! May I interrupt?

2. **Je regarde seulement. Merci.** I'm just looking. Thanks.

3. **Le rayon des chaussures, s'il vous plaît?** Where's the shoe department, please?

4. **Je ne trouve pas ma taille.** I can't find my size.

5. **C'est trop grand. Vous l'avez en plus petit?** It's too big. Do you have a smaller size?

6. **Vous n'auriez pas un autre modèle?** Would you have another style?

7. **Ce n'est pas ce que je cherchais.** It's not what I was looking for.

8. **Je voudrais réfléchir.** I'd like to think it over. (**Je ne peux pas me décider.** I can't make up my mind.)

9. **Je voudrais essayer ceci. Où est le salon d'essayage, s'il vous plaît?** I'd like to try this on. Where's the dressing room, please?

10. **C'est combien?** (Or **Ça fait combien?**) How much is it?

Ça va comme ça

There's a special kind of talk in the market. The words have to fit the melody. *Ça va comme ça* means "that's about the right amount." At the market I never hear *Combien sont les carottes?* but rather *C'est combien les carottes?* And I'm more likely to hear *Combien je vous dois?* for "How much do I owe you?" rather than *Combien est-ce que je vous dois?* Rather than «*Mes pommes sont bonnes!*» *la marchande* cries, «*Elles sont bonnes, mes pommes!*»

It's a good idea to get a feeling for what sort of quantity to ask for. *Un kilo de pommes de terre*, 2.2 pounds, is fine for potatoes. Otherwise you may want to ask for *une livre (500 grammes)*, about a pound of something.

Certain quantities tend to go with certain types of food, so it helps to learn a quantity along with an example: *un litre d'huile d'olive*, "a liter of olive oil"; *une bouteille d'eau minérale*, "a bottle of mineral water"; *un pot de moutarde*, "a pot of mustard"; *un kilo de pommes de terre*, "a couple of pounds of potatoes"; *une livre de petits pois*, "a pound of peas"; *une demi-livre de framboises*, "about half a pound of raspberries"; *une tranche de rosbif*, "a slice of roast beef"; *une douzaine d'huîtres*, "a dozen oysters"; *une botte de carottes*, "a bunch of carrots"; *une tête de laitue*, "a head of lettuce"; *une motte de beurre*, "a block of butter"; and *un morceau de fromage*, "a piece of cheese."

You could ask, *Pourriez-vous me donner un sac, s'il vous plaît?* but it's better to bring your own bag, backpack, or *un panier à provisions*, a flat-bottomed shopping basket.

TOP TEN   Things to Say at the Market

1. **C'est combien les cerises?** How much are the cherries?

2. **Je prendrai une livre. Un peu moins, s'il vous plaît.** I'd like (about) a pound. A little less, please.

3. **Et un kilo de pommes de terre.** And (about) two pounds of potatoes.

4. **Une tranche de jambon, s'il vous plaît. Un peu plus épaisse/fine.** A slice of ham, please. A little thicker/thinner.

5. **Pourriez-vous me donner un sac?** Could you give me a bag?

6. **Je prendrai quelques pêches. C'est parfait.** I'd like a few peaches. That's perfect.

7. **C'est bon. Ça va comme ça.** That's about right. That's enough.

8. **C'est pour après-demain.** They're for the day after tomorrow.

9. **Elles sont mûres?** Are they ripe? (about something with the feminine gender like tomatoes or peaches)

10. **Combien je vous dois, s'il vous plaît?** How much is that, please?

J'ai été coupé

When we talk on the phone we can't use body language, so it's no wonder that phone conversations in another language bring high anxiety. For many, using the telephone can be the most challenging part of speaking French. Things can go wrong and often do. Fortunately the French phone system works well now, so the technical part of using the telephone in France is easy.

To use public phones you need *une télécarte*, which you can buy at *un tabac*. When you enter *la cabine* to use the phone, the screen will prompt you, using infinitives to give orders: *Décrocher. Introduire carte ou faire numéro libre*; *Fermer le volet, S.V.P. Patienter.* (Then the number of units left on your card will appear on the screen.) *Numéroter: numéro appelé.* (After you dial, the number you dialed will appear on the screen and your call will go through.) When you have finished your call *le solde*, the amount left on your card, will appear on the screen.

Here's the French you need if something goes wrong when you make a phone call.

TOP TEN Telephone Problems

1. **Mon portable ne marche plus.** My cell phone's not working anymore.

2. **Je n'ai pas de télécarte.** I don't have a phone card.

3. **La cabine est occupée.** The phone booth is in use.

4. **Ça ne répond pas.** There's no answer.

5. **Elle n'est pas là.** She's not there.

6. **La ligne est occupée.** The line is busy.

7. **Je me suis trompé(e) de numéro.** I got the wrong number.

8. **J'ai été coupé(e).** I was cut off.

9. **Il est en ligne.** He's on another line.

10. **J'entends mal.** I can hardly hear you.

Ne quittez pas

Since *le portable*, "cell phone," has become a staple of French life in French cities, phone conversations among friends have become more slangy and casual. In offices and other more formal settings, the basic short phone conversation remains highly codified. *Ne quittez pas* and *Vous voulez laisser un message?* have been uttered countless times on automatic pilot.

Allô allô or just *allô* is phone talk for "Hello" in the vestigial sense of "Can you hear me?" It's a holdover from the days of bad connections. You say *bonjour* as usual when you reach the person you want to speak to. "This is Anne speaking" would be *C'est Anne à l'appareil*. When someone answers, the person may say *C'est moi*, "It's me." While it would be technically correct to say "It is I" in English, *C'est moi* is grammatically correct in French.

A couple of the stock telephone expressions are helpful for practicing word order with pronouns in a natural way. If the person you are calling is home, you hear *Je vous le passe* or *Je vous la passe*, "I'll put him on," or "I'll put her on." If you need to call back, you use expressions with *rappeler*, saying for example, *Je vais le rappeler demain* or *Je vais la rappeler demain*.

If you think you will get *le répondeur*, "the answering machine," you may want to practice the message that you will leave after hearing something like: *Vous êtes bien chez les Martin. Nous sommes absents pour le moment. Soyez gentil de laisser un message après le bip sonore.*

TOP TEN Telephone Lines

1. **Allô.** Hello.

2. **Je voudrais parler à (Madame Martin), s'il vous plaît.** I'd like to speak with (Mrs. Martin), please.

3. **C'est de la part de qui?** Who may I say is calling?

4. **Je pense qu'elle n'est pas là. Je vais m'en assurer.** I don't think she's there. I'll check.

5. **Vous voulez laisser un message?** Would you like to leave a message?

6. **Je vais la rappeler demain.** I'll call her back tomorrow.

7. **Ne quittez pas.** Just a moment.

8. **Je vous la passe.** I'll put her on.

9. **Qui est à l'appareil?** Who's calling?

10. **C'est moi, (Dominique).** It's me, (Dominique).

Le Cyber Café

Communications in France are up-to-date, and *le Cyber Café*, the Internet Café, has brought new convenience to travel. Internet cafés have sprung up all over Paris, particularly in the *quartier latin* where most of the students are. For Americans, an e-mail home has largely replaced the long-distance phone call. At a *Cyber Café* you can pay by the hour and you can also ask for a monthly rate, which gives you ten hours of service and an e-mail address.

The French invented *le minitel*, a terminal that modernized the phone system before being largely replaced by the Internet. With computers, the French use *le clavier azerty*, "the azerty keyboard." The first time you use a keyboard in France, you may find you've typed a lot of nonsense because the fingering is different.

La puce (literally, "flea") is used in expressions like *la puce électronique*, "microchip"; *la puce mémoire*, "the memory chip"; and *la carte à puce*, "the smart card."

Computer language includes some French vocabulary: *la disquette*, "floppy disk"; *le disque dur*, "hard disk"; *la base des données*, "database"; and *le listage*, "printout"—along with some would-be French vocabulary. The French terms for "e-mail"—*le courriel, le courrier électronique*, and *le mél*—are heard less often than *un e-mail*.

TOP TEN for Techies

1. **Qu'avez-vous comme ordinateur?** What kind of computer do you use?

2. **Est-ce que c'est compatible avec ce logiciel?** Is it compatible with this software?

3. **J'aimerais m'en servir pour faire du traitement de texte.** I'd like to use it for word processing.

4. **D'habitude je me sers d'un portable.** I usually use a laptop. (*Un portable* can be either a laptop or a cell phone, depending on the context.)

5. **Je voudrais me servir d'un clavier qwerty si vous en avez, s'il vous plaît.** I'd like to use a qwerty (English) keyboard if you have one, please.

6. **Je dois me servir d'une imprimante.** I need to use a printer.

7. **Vous avez une adresse électronique?** Do you have an e-mail address?

8. **Quel est votre numéro de fax?** What's your fax number?

9. **Le fax est occupé?** Is the fax being used?

10. **J'ai du mal à passer le fax.** I'm having a hard time getting the fax through.

Au secours!

Au secours! is seen more often in comic strips than it's heard in real life. *Au voleur!* is more apt to be heard in Molière's play, *L'Avare*, than on the street. Expressions to use in emergencies are some of the most essential but rarely used expressions. You will probably never use some of these expressions, but you want to have them when you need them.

The first five expressions are cries for help. The next two are expressions to use if you are bothered in the street. The classic responses are: *Laissez-moi tranquille! Allez-vous en!* and *Fichez-moi la paix!* It may be more effective to say nothing, avoid eye contact, keep moving, and ignore unwanted attention.

Sauve qui peut! is a very old expression calling on people to disband and to look out for themselves. It means literally, "Let each person get out of trouble whoever can."

TOP TEN Things You Hope Not to Have to Say

1. **Au voleur!** Stop thief!

2. **Au feu!** Fire!

3. **Au secours!** Help!

4. **Aidez-moi, s'il vous plaît. Je suis malade.** Please help me. I'm sick.

5. **Appelez un médecin! Appelez une ambulance!** Call a doctor! Call an ambulance!

6. **Laissez-moi tranquille!** Leave me alone!

7. **Allez-vous en!** Go away.

8. **On a forcé notre voiture.** Someone broke into our car.

9. **Il y a eu un accident.** There's been an accident.

10. **Sauve qui peut!** Run for your life!

Rehearsal Time

Complete the dialogues.

A la gare:

1. Je voudrais un _____-retour pour Paris, s'il vous plaît. Pour le train de 13h32. En seconde.

2. Fumeurs?
   Non. Non-fumeurs, s'il vous plaît.
   Bon. Une place en _____. Non-fumeurs. Voilà votre billet.

3. Il y a un _____-restaurant?
   Oui. Il y en a un.

4. Où est-ce que je dois _____ le billet, s'il vous plaît?
   Par là. En face, avant d'aller sur le quai.
   Merci, monsieur.

5. Excusez-moi, madame. C'est le bon _____ pour Paris?
   Oui, madame.

A l'hôtel:

6. Vous avez une chambre pour ce soir?
   Oui. Il nous reste quelques chambres. Qu'est-ce qu'il vous faut? Une chambre individuelle ou une chambre pour deux personnes? Avec salle de bains ou avec _____?

7. Une chambre pour deux personnes avec salle de bains. Si possible, une chambre tranquille qui donne sur la _____.

8. Vous allez dormir sur les deux oreilles, monsieur. Avec deux lits ou avec un _____ lit?

9. Avec deux lits. Nous avons dû laisser la voiture dans la rue. Vous avez un _____?

10. Oui, c'est derrière l'hôtel. Et le petit déjeuner est _____ dans le prix de la chambre.

Au magasin:

11. Vous désirez?
    Je _____ seulement.

12. C'est à _____?
    C'est à moi. Est-ce que je pourrais essayer cette robe, s'il vous plaît?

13. Oui, madame. Le _____ est au fond du magasin. C'est par là.

14. Ça fait _____?
    120 euros.
    Je la prends.

15. Vous allez payer comment?

    _____

Au téléphone:

16. Allô.

Allô? Qui est à _____?

C'est Dominique Lapierre. Je voudrais parler à François Lenormand.

17. Ne _____ pas.

18. Je vous le _____.

19. Il est en _____. Vous voulez laisser un message?

20. Non, je vais le _____ plus tard.

Table Talk

Learn French While Eating and Drinking
the French Way, the World's Most
Enjoyable Way of Learning by Doing

Preview

1. What is *le savoir-vivre*?

2. What kind of food could you expect at *un routier*? At *une brasserie*?

3. What's the difference between *un bistro* and *un restaurant*?

4. What is *un croque-monsieur*, and where would you expect to find one?

5. What phrase do French waiters use for "Are you ready to order?"

6. Give an example of a regional French food.

7. How do you ask for the check?

8. What would you say to call a waitress? Why?

9. How do you order "regular coffee"?

10. What should you order if you like relatively weak coffee?

11. What do you get if you order *une noisette* at a *café*?

12. If you were serving a meal, what would you say to urge your guests to have a second helping?

13. How would you say, "Can I drive you home?"

14. How do you say "no" using another word than *non* if you don't want a second helping?

15. What is another way to say in French *On le boit frais*?

16. When would you say *A vos amours*?

17. What can you say if you enjoyed a meal?

18. How do you politely announce that it's time to leave?

19. What's the special expression for "a cheap little red wine"?

20. In the context of eating and drinking, explain what's meant by *On regarde la robe*.

A guaranteed way to improve your French is to eat and drink the French way. And this is the most enjoyable way to learn by doing.

De Gaulle used to say he had a vision, *une certaine idée de la France*. Basically all of the French have *une certaine idée* of the

French meal. While many everyday French meals are becoming more like many quick and simple American ones, people of all social classes care about food and go to a great deal of trouble to plan festive meals for special occasions. Food and wine are to be appreciated with all of your senses. In any case, associating taste and sound is an excellent way to remember French idioms about food. Talking while tasting will help you remember French expressions, and having a conversation is part of the experience of the meal. A French holiday meal is still a ceremonious event, an entertainment, and a lengthy pastime.

At the heart of the special French attitude toward food is the French concept of *l'artisanat*. The artisans who make cheese, bread, and pastries may get awards such as *meilleur ouvrier de France*, "best worker, most skilled artisan in France." Artisans are less controversial and often more respected than the president. The workers who prepare French specialties in the time-honored way earn the highest respect if not the highest salaries. *Le Guide France* talks about food as involving *un code et une méthode, des principes, des lois, des aphorismes... la célébration d'un rite et une œuvre d'art* "a code and a method, principles, laws, aphorisms . . . the celebration of a rite and a work of art."

Many of the French food rules are based on scientific knowledge about nutrition and digestion. For this reason, ways of eating that Americans consider a matter of personal preference can be considered "wrong" in France. The negative ideas that Americans sometimes have about the French can often be traced to experiences with inflexible French waiters who want to deal with food according to French traditions. Some Americans go to France for the food but then get upset when waiters don't do things the American way.

Even the simplest of meals can be memorable—a picnic in a park with a baguette, some butter, and ripe tomatoes, or perhaps some take-out food from *une charcuterie*, and a bottle of wine and *un tire-bouchon*, "a corkscrew."

Having a traditional French meal is as much about *savoir-vivre*, etiquette, as it's about food. If you break the rules, it's assumed that you don't know them, because the idea is to become better at eating and drinking rather than to eat whatever you please.

When in France, you should either eat the French way or be prepared for the consequences. But many Americans don't think of eating as a skill. From the French perspective, you have to learn to be good at eating.

The French may poke fun at political correctness, but they take their food seriously. When it comes to food, even those who may have an insouciant attitude toward dogma in other contexts show true devotion to the rules. To a certain extent food still rules the lives of the French. Much of Sunday can be spent at the table with relatives. Holidays tend to be organized around food.

Just as you have to learn a lot of French idioms before you can speak French creatively, you have to learn the French rules of gastronomic correctness before you can decide whether or not it's worth breaking them. Fortunately, most people end up enjoying French meals even more as they learn about French ways of eating.

French Table Manners

Do you already understand French table manners? The following quiz will let you check your *savoir-vivre*. The point here is not to say that the French way is better. You may choose not to do things the French way. What's important is to know the written and unwritten rules so that you can be aware of what you're doing in relation to them. If you decide to break the rules, at least you know what you're doing.

Choose one or more answers to each question. You can check your answers against the Answer Key.

1. How do the French use a fork?
   a. They keep the fork in the left hand.
   b. They keep the fork in the right hand.
   c. They switch from right to left.
   d. They switch from left to right.

2. What do the French do with a napkin?
   a. If their mouths are wet they wipe their mouths with the napkins before drinking.
   b. They wipe the glasses before drinking.
   c. They leave the napkins beside the plates during the meal.
   d. They put the napkins on their laps.

3. Which of the following should not be ordered with a meal?
   a. Coca-Cola
   b. iced tea
   c. tea
   d. coffee

4. To order water the French say:
   a. *un Évian*
   b. *un Perrier*
   c. *un verre d'eau avec un glaçon* "A glass of water with ice"
   d. *une carafe d'eau* "A pitcher of water"

5. The best all-purpose wine glass is:
   a. *la tulipe*, similar in shape to that of the tulip
   b. *la flûte*, with sides that do not curve in at the top
   c. *le ballon*, a round glass that looks as though the top of a sphere had been cut off
   d. *la coupe*, a wide and shallow glass

6. Acceptable topics of conversation include:
   a. books, plays, movies
   b. philosophical and ethical dilemmas
   c. personal life
   d. religion and salary

7. During a meal the French do not:
   a. put their hands on the table
   b. put their hands in their laps
   c. put their forearms on the edge of the table
   d. eat with their fingers

8. When eating bread the French:
   a. always insist on a bread-and-butter plate
   b. keep their bread on the tablecloth
   c. always use butter

9. The French eat their soup:
   a. by gently sipping from the bowl
   b. from the tip of the spoon
   c. from the side of the spoon
   d. by dipping bread in it

10. At a restaurant, the French eat an apple or a pear:
    a. with their fingers
    b. by cutting it in four with a knife and then eating it with their fingers
    c. with a knife and fork
    d. with a knife and spoon

11. When the French take some cheese they:
    a. cut off a piece so that the remaining piece retains the general shape it had before they cut their piece
    b. cut off a piece from the middle
    c. cut off a piece from the end nearest them

12. When choosing cheese as dessert the French:
    a. always try more than three cheeses from the platter
    b. take four cheeses as a general rule
    c. don't take more than three cheeses

13. When helping themselves to part of a baguette the French:
    a. pull off a piece of bread from a baguette with their fingers
    b. cut the bread with a knife while holding one end with a dish towel
    c. never eat the end piece

14. For the salad the French:
    a. ask for French dressing
    b. ask for low-fat dressing

c. ask for blue-cheese dressing

d. don't specify a dressing

15. To eat a big piece of lettuce the French:
    a. cut the lettuce with a knife
    b. use the edge of the fork to cut it
    c. fold the lettuce using a knife and fork and eat it with a fork
    d. cut it into very small pieces

16. To order coffee after lunch or dinner the French say:
    a. *un café au lait*
    b. *un grand crème*
    c. *un express*
    d. *un café*
    e. *un café avec du lait*
    f. *un déca*

17. After the meal the French leave their napkins:
    a. folded above the plate
    b. unfolded to the left of the plate
    c. folded and to the right of the plate
    d. unfolded on the chair

18. To show that they have finished, the French leave the knife and fork:
    a. parallel on the plate at five o'clock
    b. on the plate at six o'clock with the fork upside down
    c. facing each other across the plate
    d. in the shape of an *accent circonflexe* on the plate

On va prendre un repas

When you are offered something to eat or drink you are usually asked with a form of *prendre* what you will "take." If you reply with a verb, it tends to be *prendre*. *On prend quelque chose.*

In French *On prend les repas*—without the verb *manger*. You *take* your meals, you don't *eat* them. *On prend le déjeuner et le dîner.* You can eat something specific though. *On peut manger du pain ou un fruit.*

It's still traditional for adults to have a big midday Sunday meal at their parents' or grandparents' house as seen in Bertrand Tavernier's 1984 movie, *Un dimanche à la campagne*, and in Merchant-Ivory's 2003 film, *Le Divorce*.

Restaurants serve full meals. Other varieties of restaurant are *le bistro*, an intimate eating place with a smaller menu, and *la brasserie*, known for beer but also serving basic meals such as *un steak frites*, "steak and fries." *Une auberge* is a restaurant in a country inn or in an old and attractive building.

Un routier is a truck stop, often serving hearty and reasonably priced meals. (*Un routier* is also a truck driver.) At *un snack-bar* you can eat sandwiches standing up or sitting on a high stool at a counter.

Un bar serves beer, wine, hard liquor, and soft drinks as well as coffee. You can also count on a few simple sandwiches, such as *un sandwich au jambon* and *un sandwich au fromage*. *Le café* is known for its tables on the sidewalk. You can ask to sit *à la terrasse* or *dehors*, outside, or *à l'intérieur*. *Le café* serves mostly coffee and other drinks and has a few sandwiches such as *le croque-monsieur* and *le croque-madame*. Both *le croque-monsieur* and *le croque-madame* are toasted ham-and-cheese sandwiches, but *le croque-madame* sometimes has a fried egg on top. In some versions *le croque-madame* includes chicken instead of ham—and then there's no fried egg.

TOP TEN Places for a Meal

1. **On peut prendre quelque chose *chez moi*.** We can have something to eat at my house.

2. **On peut prendre le repas de dimanche *chez mes parents*.** We can have Sunday lunch at my parents' house.

3. **On peut prendre le dîner *au restaurant*.** We can have dinner at a restaurant.

4. **On peut prendre le souper *au bistro* après le spectacle.** We can have supper at a bistro after the show.

5. **On peut prendre une omelette *dans une brasserie*.** We can have an omelet at a brasserie.

6. **On peut prendre le déjeuner *dans une auberge*.** We can have lunch at a rustic restaurant.

7. **On peut déjeuner *dans un routier*.** We can have lunch at a truck stop.

8. **On peut prendre un casse-croûte *dans un snack-bar*.** We can have a snack or a light lunch at a snack bar.

9. **On peut prendre un verre et un sandwich *dans un bar*.** We can get a drink and a sandwich at a bar.

10. **On peut prendre un croque-monsieur *au café*.** We can have a toasted ham and cheese sandwich at a café.

Monsieur! Mademoiselle!

One of the best known French expressions among those who have studied French as a second language is *Garçon!* (literally, "Boy!") as a way to call a waiter. *Ça ne se dit plus.* This isn't said any more and French waiters don't like it. You can say *Monsieur!* or *S'il vous plaît!* or gesture—as long as you don't say *Garçon!* The French consciousness has not yet been raised with regard to female wait staff, though. They are still summoned by *Mademoiselle!* "Miss!" no matter what their age or marital status, even though French women, married or single, are otherwise politely called *Madame*.

A waiter may ask you *Avez-vous déjà commandé?* "Has someone already taken your order?" or *Vous allez commander?* "Are you ready to order?" When you order you can say *Je voudrais commander le saumon*, "I'd like to order the salmon." It's not necessary to repeat the verb *commander*. You can also start your reply with *Je vais pren-*

dre: Je vais prendre le saumon. You can also just say *Je voudrais le saumon* or *Le saumon, s'il vous plaît.*

A 15 percent tip is usually included in the price of a meal, and you'll see *service compris* printed on the bill. If not, you can ask, *Le service est compris?* If it isn't, leave a 15 percent tip and consider it part of the price of the meal. It's not optional. If the service charge is included you still usually leave some change on the table. The philosophy of tipping can vary from person to person. Suggestions have included: leave small change on the table; always leave a couple of euros on the table; leave an additional 2–3 percent; always leave an additional 5 percent.

TOP TEN Expressions for Talking with French Waiters

1. **On est quatre.** There are four of us.

2. **Qu'est-ce que vous proposez aujourd'hui?** What do you suggest today?

3. **Quelles sont les spécialités de la maison?** What are the specials?

4. **La carte des vins, s'il vous plaît.** The wine list, please.

5. **Nous allons prendre le menu.** We'll have the fixed-price meal.

6. **Je n'arrive pas à me décider entre le saumon et le cassoulet.** I can't decide between the salmon and the cassoulet.

7. **Quel vin est-ce que vous me recommandez pour accompagner cela?** What wine do you recommend to go with that?

8. **Monsieur!** Waiter!

9. **L'addition, s'il vous plaît.** The check, please.

10. **Le service est compris?** Is the tip included?

Les amuse-gueule et les hors-d'œuvre

The parts of a French meal can be confusing. Some parts of the meal have tricky names, such as *les amuse-gueule* and *les hors-d'œuvre*. Even words such as *l'entrée* that are the same in English can refer to a different part of the meal than you'd expect. In French, *l'entrée* is the course that opens up the meal for the main course, *le plat*. Even in French, *l'entrée* can be confusing because it is used both ways. Use the quiz below to help you put things in order. Choose one or more answers to each question. You can check your answers in the Answer Key.

Le repas

1. *L'apéritif* is:
   a. a drink taken before lunch or dinner that stimulates the appetite
   b. a wine such as *porto*
   c. a wine such as *lillet* or *kir*

2. *Les amuse-gueule* are:
   a. nuts and small crackers served with the *apéritif* in the living room before the meal
   b. an appetizer served at the table as the first course
   c. sharp spreads such as horseradish

3. *Les hors-d'œuvre* are:
   a. nuts and nibbles
   b. the first course, such as a soup
   c. brie and other French cheeses served with crackers and grapes

4. *L'entrée* is:
   a. the main course
   b. the course before the main course
   c. the course after the main course

5. *Le plat* or *le plat de résistance* is:
   a. the plate
   b. the main course
   c. the most delicious course

6. *La salade* is served:
   a. before the main course
   b. after the main course
   c. with the main course, in a separate bowl

7. *La salade* is usually composed of:
   a. just lettuce and vinaigrette
   b. lettuce, tomato, cucumber, and one or two other vegetables depending on the season
   c. lettuce, cucumber, onion, and herbs

8. *Le fromage*:
   a. should always be served with a great wine
   b. should be served with wine
   c. should never be served with wine

9. *Le café* is served:
   a. during the meal
   b. with dessert
   c. after dessert

10. *Le digestif (le pousse-café)* is served:
    a. before the meal
    b. after the meal
    c. with the meal

How did you do? Here's a summary of the stages of the French meal along with some of the verbs that go with food and drink.

TOP TEN Stages of a French Meal

1. **On prend** *l'apéritif.* We have an aperitif.

2. **On goûte les** *amuse-gueule.* We taste the appetizers.

3. **On commence par les** *hors-d'œuvre.* We start with the first course.

4. **On apprécie l'***entrée.* We enjoy the second course.

5. **On raffole du** *plat.* We're crazy about the main course.

6. **On mange de la** *salade.* We eat some salad.

7. **On se sert de** *fromage.* We help ourselves to cheese.

8. **On commande le** *dessert.* We order dessert.

9. **On boit du** *café.* We drink coffee.

10. **On savoure le** *digestif* **ou le** *pousse-café.* We savor the liqueur.

Qu'est-ce que vous prendrez?

The French particularly enjoy fresh foods that are in season and local specialties. When they travel they try the specialties of the region and the local wines. Follow their lead and you too will learn more about French food.

Many French specialties are named after the town or region they come from. *Le roquefort* comes from Roquefort, *le camembert* from Camembert, *l'armagnac* from Armagnac, and *le champagne* from la Champagne. French regional cooking is a huge subject. To suggest a few specialties as well as those named below, *la bouillabaisse*, "fish stew," comes from Marseille; *le coq au vin* comes from la Bourgogne, *la tarte tatin*, "upside-down apple pie," comes from la Normandie; and *les crêpes* and *le cidre* from la Bretagne.

Although the French usually have meat as a main course, it's almost always possible for a vegetarian to find some delicious vegetable and fruit dishes on the menu. To say what you'd like, you can use the words *volontiers* and *bien* as follows: *Je prendrais volontiers du melon*. "I'd be glad to have some melon." *Je prendrais bien des champignons farcis*. "I'd really like some stuffed mushrooms."

If you don't want to have any melon, you say, *Merci. Je ne prends pas de melon* (pronounced *pas d'melon*). Similarly, you'd say *pas de champignons* (*pas d'champignons*). But if you want to say you don't like melon, it's *Je n'aime pas le melon*. Usually you can enjoy all of the courses because the menu is well planned and the portions are small.

TOP TEN   Regional Specialties

1. **Le melon de Cavaillon.** The best melons are from Cavaillon.

2. **Le jambon de Bayonne.** The raw ham from Bayonne is prized.

3. **Les champignons farcis à la périgourdine.** Le Périgord is known for mushrooms stuffed with truffles and *foie gras*.

4. **L'agneau à la provençale.** Roast lamb with baked tomatoes, garlic, and mushrooms as prepared in Provence.

5. **Le cassoulet toulousain.** A specialty of Toulouse, this casserole dish is made with a base of white beans and a variety of meats.

6. **La brandade de Nîmes.** Mashed potatoes mixed with desalted codfish, olive oil, and garlic, a specialty of Nîmes.

7. **Le roquefort.** On *le plateau de fromages*, "the cheese tray," you choose a couple of cheeses. *Le roquefort* comes from Roquefort.

8. **Marrons à la lyonnaise.** Purée of chestnuts in the style of Lyon.

9. **La tarte normande aux pommes.** An open-faced pie made of apples and custard that's a specialty of Normandie.

10. **Le clafoutis limousin.** A cherry flan that's a specialty of Limousin.

Un grand crème

An American teacher visiting Paris had been trying unsuccessfully for several mornings to order a cup of coffee with milk in it at a *café*. When he had asked for *un café avec du lait* he received a demi-tasse cup with an inch of espresso and a small pitcher of steamed milk. One day he happened to be sitting next to a Frenchman who was drinking a cup of coffee with milk in it—just what he had been trying to order. «*Excusez-moi, monsieur. Qu'est-ce que c'est?*» he asked, pointing to the coffee. «*Mais c'est un café,*» said the French-man, astonished at being asked such an obvious question. «*Mais qu'est-ce que vous avez dit pour le commander?*» asked the American. Ah, he smiled, *un grand crème*.

Un grand crème is not the sort of expression you would guess by trial and error. First of all, *crème* is feminine and *un* and *grand* are masculine. Even if you reconstitute the whole expression, *Je vais prendre un grand café avec de la crème*, it's not completely logical to Americans, because milk is used more often than cream, and the cup does not look big.

American coffee is disparaged by the French as *du jus de chaus-settes*, "sock juice." If you want to order American coffee you can try asking for *un café allongé*, weak coffee, thinned down, "length-ened" with added water.

Coffee is only ordered with milk in the morning. *Un café au lait* is good with *un croissant* or a piece of *baguette*. Alternatively, it's possible to have *un crème* (in an espresso cup) or *un grand crème* in the morning. Similarly, *un cappuccino* is only ordered in the morning in France, as in Italy. You could also order *une noisette*, which is an espresso with a drop of milk in it (literally, "hazelnut"). At lunch people usually order *un express* after the midday meal. In the evening, many prefer *un déca*, "decaf espresso." When you dip *un morceau de sucre*, "a sugar cube," in any kind of coffee, it's called *un canard* when it comes out. *Je prends un canard* means "I'm having a sugar cube dipped in coffee."

TOP TEN Ways to Order Coffee in France

1. **Un café au lait.** Mostly steamed milk with a little coffee.

2. **Un crème.** An espresso with steamed milk served in an espresso cup.

3. **Un grand crème.** Espresso with steamed milk served in a standard-sized cup.

4. **Une noisette.** An espresso with a drop of milk in it. The drop of milk gives the coffee a hazelnut color.

5. **Un express.** About an inch of espresso in a very small cup.

6. **Un café, un café noir.** Other words for espresso.

7. **Un café serré.** A very strong espresso.

8. **Un double express.** A double espresso.

9. **Un café allongé.** Weak coffee.

10. **Un déca.** Decaf espresso.

Encore un peu?

A formal meal at a restaurant or at someone's home can have much in common with an evening at the theater. While the conversation may be unpredictable, the evening itself has various scenes according to the various stages of the meal. When you are first asked, *Qu'est-ce que vous prenez?* this refers to what you'd like to drink as an *apéritif*. Since your host may or may not have a wide selection, it's always polite to reply *Qu'est-ce que vous me proposez?* "What do you suggest?" Some possibilities are *le kir, le vermouth, le dubonnet, le lillet,* and *le pastis.*

One way to announce dinner is *On va se mettre à table,* "We'll go to the table." Another, more formal, way is *Le dîner est servi.* Your host may or may not say *Bon appétit,* but if you are drinking wine, there will probably be a toast. The generic toasts are variations on *A votre santé,* "to your health," or *A vos amours* (literally, "to your loves"). But usually there's something specific to toast. At someone's house you'll drink to your friendship or to any recent good news.

TOP TEN Lines of the Host or Hostess

1. **Quel plaisir de vous voir.** It's good to see you.

2. **Qu'est-ce que vous prenez?** What will you have to drink?

3. **Le dîner est servi.** Dinner is served.

4. **Asseyez-vous donc.** Come and sit down.

5. **A notre amitié.** To our friendship.

6. **Vous en reprendrez bien un peu?** Have some more.

7. **Servez-vous.** Please help yourself. **Si vous voulez bien reprendre des petits pois.** Please, have more peas.

8. **Vous ne voulez pas rester encore un moment avec nous?** Can't you stay a little while longer?

9. **Vous nous quittez si tôt?** You're leaving us already?

10. **Je peux vous raccompagner?** Can I drive you home?

Quelle réussite!

Exclamations about a good meal include *Quelle réussite!* and *Comme c'est bon! Comme c'est délicieux!* When accepting a serving or a second helping, you can say *Avec plaisir* and *Volontiers*. When refusing, it's customary to say *Merci*, meaning no—so it's important not to say *merci* by itself if you'd like something you're offered.

If you're offered a ride home you can say *C'est très gentil* or *Si ça ne vous dérange pas trop* for yes and *Ce n'est pas la peine* for no. *On a la voiture* is what you say if you drove there.

TOP TEN Lines of the Guest

In appreciation of the meal:

1. **C'est délicieux. Merveilleux.** It's delicious. Marvelous.

2. **Quelle réussite!** This turned out very well. (What a success!)

3. **Avec plaisir.** Yes. With pleasure. (when offered a second helping)

4. **Merci. C'était très bon.** No thank you, it was very good. (when refusing a second helping)

5. **Juste un petit peu, s'il vous plaît.** Just a little, please.

When taking leave:

6. **Il se fait tard. Il est temps de rentrer.** It's getting late. It's time to go home.

7. **Nous avons passé une très bonne soirée.** We had a very good time.

8. **Au revoir. J'espère qu'on se reverra bientôt.** Good-bye. I hope we'll see you soon.

When offered a ride:

9. **C'est très gentil si ça ne vous dérange pas trop.** That would be very nice if it's not too much trouble.

10. **Non merci, on a la voiture.** No thanks, we drove here.

Ce qui se fait

Rules about food and wine tend to start with *on* or use reflexive verbs like *se manger* and *se boire. On le boit frais* or *Ça se boit frais.* The reflexive construction seems a good match for rules about food and drink because the classic expressions of this type are *Ça se fait*, "It's what's done," and *Ça se dit*, "It's what's said."

You usually pour a little wine in the bottom of your glass so that you can taste it and see if it's good before everyone has some. If you're in a restaurant, the wine should not be sent back unless you really know what you are doing.

Although in France you are generally not supposed to eat or drink anything very hot or very cold, champagne is the exception. Since champagne should be kept coldest of all wines, almost at freezing temperature, it is kept in a pail of ice near the table. Champagne is also an exception in that it can go with anything and with any stage of the meal.

Great red wines should be brought to room temperature. Bourgogne and bordeaux that are aged more than about ten years should be uncorked an hour or more before the meal so that they can breathe at room temperature. Young red wines can be opened just before serving.

Usually when there's more than one wine, a white is served before a red, and a red before champagne. A maximum of three different wines should be served during a formal meal.

TOP TEN Rules of Serving Wine

1. **On se verse un fond de verre.** Pour a little wine in the bottom of your glass.

2. **Les vins rosés se servent frais.** Rosés should be chilled.

3. **Les vins blancs secs se servent très frais.** Dry white wines should be well chilled.

4. **Le champagne se sert frappé.** Champagne should be very well chilled.

5. **Les grands vins se laissent chambrer.** Great wines should be brought to room temperature.

6. **Le vin blanc sec se boit avec le poisson.** Dry white wine goes with fish.

7. **Le vin rouge se boit avec la viande.** Red wine goes with meat.

8. **Le rosé se boit au déjeuner ou avec une salade.** You have rosé with lunch or a salad.

9. **Un vin doux se boit avec le dessert.** A sweet wine goes with dessert.

10. **On ne doit jamais servir plus de trois vins pendant un repas.** You should never serve more than three different wines with a meal.

On hume le vin

To appreciate a wine, you need to use your taste buds, but also your eyes and your nose. First you hold the wine up to the light to see *la robe*, which is the color—its intensity, density, and reflection. Then you swish it around a little: *On laisse se développer le bouquet.* You let it develop a nose, and you smell it gently for the bouquet.

The expression, *Ce vin a de la mâche* means that the wine feels good when you first take it in your mouth. You let the wine warm up a little in your mouth before tasting it. When you taste the wine, you try to place the various scents and flavors. Taste is subjective, but in general a fine wine is full-bodied but not too heavy, subtle but not dull, light but not thin. *Il est équilibré.* "It's balanced."

TOP TEN Stages of Tasting of Wine

1. **On regarde la robe.** You look at the color of the wine.

2. **On tourne le vin très doucement dans le verre.** You swish it around a few times very gently in the glass.

3. **On hume le vin.** You smell the wine.

4. **On prend une petite gorgée et on la fait rouler dans la bouche.** You take a little sip and swish it around in your mouth.

5. **On n'avale pas tout de suite.** You don't swallow right away.

6. **On reconnaît les arômes.** You recognize (place) the scents.

7. **On avale une petite gorgée.** You take a little sip.

8. **On goûte le vin.** You taste the wine.

9. **On reconnaît les saveurs.** You recognize the flavors.

10. **On se prononce.** You say what you think of the wine.

Il n'est pas long en bouche

It is really pretentious to talk about French wine if you don't know anything about the subject. On the other hand, talking about wine as a way of trying to learn about it is not pretentious. Wine making is an art, and many people approach it with an aesthetic interest. Most of the people who really know about wine have an attitude of humility even as they talk extensively about it.

If you are not familiar with French wines, ask the waiter's advice on which wines would go well with the meal. He or she should be able and willing to propose several at different prices. You can educate your palate by trying different wines and learning about wine, but you will still have personal preferences.

Here are some of the guidelines that the French follow: Glasses should not be left empty, but they should not be filled more than two-thirds full. Wine's best without water or cigarettes. You are supposed to avoid serving a fine wine with food such as raw onions, garlic, mustard, or vinegar, which might interfere with the taste of the wine. If a wine is good but not great it can best be enjoyed with food. If you are lucky enough to taste a great wine it's best tasted without food.

TOP TEN Negative Comments About Wine

1. **Il n'est pas long en bouche.** The taste doesn't stay in your mouth.

2. **Il est acide.** It's acidic.

3. **Il est dur.** It's hard.

4. **Il est un peu plat.** It's a bit flat.

5. **Il est trop jeune, pas encore mûr.** It's too young, not mature yet.

6. **Il est trop lourd.** It's too heavy.

7. **C'est un petit rouge qui tache.** It's a cheap red wine. (Literally, it's a little red that stains.)

8. **Il est imbuvable.** It's undrinkable.

9. **Il tourne au vinaigre.** It's turning to vinager.

10. **C'est du picrate.** It's cheap wine.

TOP TEN Positive Comments About Wine

1. **Il est long en bouche.** It stays in your mouth. It holds its own.

2. **Il sent la violette.** It has a taste of violet.

3. **Il est mœlleux.** It's mellow.

4. **Il est élégant et complexe.** It's elegant and complex.

5. **C'est un vin mûr.** It's a mature wine.

6. **Il est souple et léger.** It's supple and light.

7. **Il sent le cassis.** It has a taste of black currant.

8. **Il sent l'amande.** It has a taste of almond.

9. **Il est fruité.** It's fruity.

10. **C'est un grand vin.** It's a great wine.

Rehearsal Time

You are a guest at someone's house. Respond to the questions asked by your host during the course of the evening.

1. Qu'est-ce que vous prenez comme apéritif?

2. Vous prendrez des champignons?

3. Vous en reprendrez bien un peu?

4. Vous ne voulez pas rester encore un moment avec nous?

5. Je peux vous raccompagner?

You arrive at a restaurant. Answer the waiter's questions. You may use the regional specialties on pages 110–111 to answer questions 8, 9, and 11.

6. Vous êtes combien?

7. Où préférez-vous vous asseoir ?

8. Pour commencer? Qu'est-ce que vous prendrez comme hors-d'œuvre?

9. Et ensuite?

10. Et comme boisson?

11. Vous désirez un dessert?

12. Du café?

You are taking a short gastronomy quiz. Answer the following questions:

13. Quels vins se servent très frais?

14. Quels vins se laissent chambrer?

15. Quel vin se sert frappé?

16. Quel vin se boit avec le poisson, en général?

17. Quel vin se boit avec le dessert?

18. Quel vin se boit au déjeuner ou avec une salade?

At a wine tasting you are asked your opinion on a couple of wines:

19. Parlez d'un vin que vous aimez. (au moins deux expressions)

20. Parlez d'un vin que vous n'aimez pas. (au moins deux expressions)

TUNE-UP
6

Conversation Starters

Ask the Questions That Will Make the French Want to Talk with You

1. In what four ways can you ask a yes-or-no question in French?

2. What's the one-word expression for "What did you say?" in French?

3. How do you ask in French how something is spelled?

4. How do you ask what something means?

5. What is meant by the question *De quoi s'agit-il au fond?*

6. How do you ask "What's the matter?"

7. In what situation is it useful to say *Où est-ce que je dois descendre?*

8. How do you ask where you can park?

9. What is *le Questionnaire Proust?*

10. How do you say "Where are you from?" in French?

11. What's the difference between *une revue* and *un magazine?*

12. What can you find out by asking the French what newspapers they read?

13. In French, how do you ask people what they do?

14. Should you ask French people what they do?

15. What is meant by *un cadre?*

16. What is meant by *la BD*, and what is its importance in France?

17. What's the difference between *un cahier* and *un carnet?*

18. What is the difference between *la TGB* and *le TGV?*

19. In what part of the francophone world does *discuter* have the same meaning as *se disputer?*

20. What's the difference between *une conversation* and *une discussion?*

One of the best ways to learn another language is to ask questions, and these questions don't always have to be about the language itself. You ask questions to communicate with people, get information, figure out what you need to know, or explore a meaning. You can also ask questions to find out what's on people's minds. You then have a chance to listen.

On the most basic level, simple everyday questions are asked and answered as social rituals. You can ask one-word questions to get more information: *Qui? Où? Comment? Quand? Pourquoi?* "Who?" "Where?" "How?" "When?" "Why?" There are polite ways that you can ask someone for help. You can ask questions to clarify information.

Open-ended questions lead you into a discussion or debate. This is the best kind of question for learning about France and for learning more about the French. You only need to figure out what you'd like to know and then dare to ask. Some of your questions may be brushed off. As long as your intention is kind, so what?

An introductory chapter about pronunciation and intonation showed how to change the pitch of your voice to ask a question. An example of this sort of question is *Il y a quelqu'un?* "Is anybody home?"

This chapter will focus primarily on the kinds of questions that don't just rely on intonation. The first list suggests the range of ways of asking questions. While it does not include all of the possible ways of asking questions, you will see as models some of the questions that will be included in the top ten lists that follow.

TOP TEN Ways to Ask Questions

1. **Est-ce que... ?** Pitch rises with *est-ce que* questions, just as it does with the conversational form *C'est loin?* You can ask, *Est-ce que c'est loin?*

2. **... n'est-ce pas?** In conversation, yes/no questions can also be asked by adding *n'est-ce pas* to the end of a statement. You could ask *C'est loin, n'est-ce pas?*

3. **Inversion.** Another way of asking a yes/no question is by inverting the order of the subject and verb: *Pourriez-vous répéter, s'il vous plaît?*

4. **Qui, Qui est-ce que, Qu'est-ce qui, Qu'est-ce que... ?** *Qui*: *Qui vous a dit cela? Qui est-ce que*: *Qui est-ce que vous avez vu? Qu'est-ce qui*: *Qu'est-ce qui ne va pas? Qu'est-ce que*: *Qu'est-ce qu'il y a?*

5. **Quel, Quelle, Quels, Quelles... ?** *Quelle est la plus belle cathédrale française à votre avis?*

6. **Où?** *Où est-ce que je dois descendre?*

7. **Comment?** *Comment est-ce que ça s'écrit?*

8. **Combien?** *Combien de temps faut-il pour y aller?*

9. **Quand?** *Quand préférez-vous partir en vacances?*

10. **Pourquoi?** *Pourquoi les Français ne font-ils pas autant de jogging que les Américains à votre avis?*

De quoi s'agit-il au fond?

Comment? can be a one-word question meaning "What did you say?" You don't need to give up right away if you don't understand either literally or figuratively what someone is telling you.

Even in English we sometimes need to ask, "What did you mean by that?" In another language this sort of question is the key to avoiding linguistic misunderstandings and cultural miscommunication. You can ask how something is written if you don't understand the words, and you can ask, *Qu'est-ce que ça veut dire?* or *De quoi s'agit-il au fond?* if you want to know what someone really means. *De quoi s'agit-il au fond?* may be more neutral than *Qu'est-ce que ça veut dire?* which can be understood to mean "What's going on here?" If you definitely do want to ask someone what he or she is getting at, you can ask *Où voulez-vous en venir?*

TOP TEN Questions for Checking Understanding

1. **Comment?** What?

2. **Pourriez-vous répéter, s'il vous plaît?** Could you say that again, please?

3. **Qu'est-ce que vous avez dit?** What did you say?

4. **Comment est-ce que ça s'écrit?** How is that spelled?

5. **Qu'est-ce que ça veut dire?** What does that mean?

6. **De quoi s'agit-il au fond?** What's this really about?

7. **Qu'est-ce qu'il y a?** What's the matter?

8. **Qu'est-ce qui ne va pas?** What's wrong?

9. **Est-ce que j'ai bien compris?** Have I understood correctly?

10. **Sommes-nous d'accord?** Do we agree?

Où est-ce que je peux garer la voiture?

When you travel, you often have to ask where things are and how to get where you're going. It's hard to acknowledge that you don't know what you're doing, and harder still to ask questions when you're not sure how to ask them. It's good to have these questions on the tip of your tongue and to always add *s'il vous plaît* when asking for help. *Je vais stationner* and *Je vais garer la voiture* both mean "I'm going to park the car." If you see *payant* marked on a street, it means you have to deposit money in a pay box or get a parking card, again from *un tabac*. Then you get a receipt from the pay box and display it in the front window of your car. When in doubt, always ask *Où est-ce que je peux garer la voiture?*

TOP TEN Questions for Getting Around

1. **Comment peut-on y aller?** How do you get there?

2. **Où faut-il aller?** Where do you have to go?

3. **Combien de temps faut-il pour y aller?** How long does it take to get there?

4. **Quelle ligne dois-je prendre?** What (subway or bus) line do I have to take?

5. **Où est-ce que je dois changer?** Where should I change?

6. **Où est-ce que je dois descendre?** Where should I get off?

7. **Est-ce que c'est loin?** Is it far?

8. **Où est-ce que je peux garer la voiture?** Where can I park?

9. **Où y a-t-il une station-service, s'il vous plaît?** Where's a gas station, please?

10. **Où est-ce que je pourrais trouver un taxi?** Where could I find a taxi?

Aimez-vous le jazz?

France has a famous set of questions for getting to know someone, the *Questionnaire Proust*. It was made famous by Proust's answers at a young age to psychological questions such as *Quel serait pour vous le comble de la misère?* "What would be the worst thing that could happen to you?" He said being separated from his mother. The questions of the *Questionnaire Proust* became a rite of passage for French celebrities. Then Bernard Pivot, who used to host a phenomenally popular literary TV show, "Apostrophes," developed a new set of celebrity questions, replacing the *Questionnaire Proust*. James Lipton, on "Inside the Actor's Studio," then asked Pivot's questions in English on American television. Finally Pivot invited Lipton to ask him his own questions on the last episode of "Apostrophes." You will see Pivot's answer to one of his own questions in Tune-Up 7. The following questions are another version of the psychological questions that may be asked to get to know someone.

Ask about jazz, if you like it. The French often know a lot about it and consider it the most important American art form of the last century. Asking people what newspapers and magazines they read is considered acceptable, while asking directly about political affiliation may not always be acceptable. It amounts to the same thing. French newspapers have clear philosophical affiliations as do *les revues*, which are news magazines, reviews, and journals. Among newspapers, for example, *L'Humanité* is the organ of the Communist Party; *Libération* is socialist; *Le Monde*, a widely admired newspaper, is somewhat on the left, although it's read by intellectuals of the left and right; and *Le Figaro* is on the right. *Les magazines* tend to be picture magazines such as *Paris-Match*, considered a rough equivalent of *People* combined with the *National Enquirer*.

TOP TEN Questions for Getting to Know Someone

1. **Comment vous appelez-vous?** What's your name?

2. **Aimez-vous le jazz?** Do you like jazz?

3. **Qu'est-ce que vous aimez lire?** What do you like to read?

4. **Faites-vous du sport?** Do you do any sports?

5. **Quelle sorte de films préférez-vous?** What kind of films do you prefer?

6. **Quand préférez-vous partir en vacances?** When do you prefer to go off on vacation?

7. **Quel/Quelle est votre acteur/actrice préféré(e)?** Who is your favorite actor?

8. **Quelles revues lisez-vous?** What magazines do you read?

9. **Quel journal lisez-vous?** What newspaper do you read?

10. **Si vous pouviez aller n'importe où dans le monde, où iriez-vous?** If you could go anywhere in the world, where would you go?

Que faites-vous dans la vie?

The French do not ask personal questions in casual conversation. Before asking a question, determine that it is appropriate and not intrusive.

Que faites-vous dans la vie? is the French way of asking "What do you do?" "What is your job?" The French do not ask it as often or as quickly in the conversation as Americans do. In French, this is usually a discreet question that can be answered lots of ways. If you're a doctor, you could say *Je suis médecin* (not *un médecin*). You say *Je fais de la médecine* only if you are in medical school.

Sometimes French jobs have cultural references that Americans aren't familiar with. For example, a lot of the French positions are called *cadres*, a term that does not have an exact equivalent in English. *Les cadres* are the managerial staff. The closest equivalent of *un cadre* in English is an executive or manager. Another French term that's used a lot is *un fonctionnaire*, "civil servant": *La plupart des professeurs sont fonctionnaires.*

When giving a phone number, the French say digits in pairs, whereas Americans say each number individually. For example, the

French phone number 01.46.27.03.24 would be said as *zéro un/quarante-six/vingt-sept/zéro trois/vingt-quatre*.

TOP TEN Personal Questions

1. **Que faites-vous dans la vie?** What's your job? What do you do?

2. **Quelle est votre situation de famille?** Are you married? Divorced? Single?

3. **Quel est votre numéro de téléphone?** What is your phone number?

4. **Quelle est votre adresse e-mail?** What's your e-mail?

5. **Quelle est votre adresse?** What's your address?

6. **Est-ce que vos parents vivent toujours?** Are your parents still alive?

7. **Est-ce que vous vous intéressez à la politique?** Are you interested in politics?

8. **D'où venez-vous?** Where are you from?

9. **Vous avez des projets pour demain?** Do you have plans for tomorrow? (if you are friends)

10. **Est-ce que je pourrais vous accompagner?** May I go with you?

Comment peut-on être français?

Montesquieu made fun of Parisians who wanted to know *Comment peut-on être persan?* "What can I do to be Persian?" (Literally, "How can one be Persian?")

The subject of what it means to be French can give rise to energetic conversations. Sometimes people prefer to give their own opinions guardedly at first, under the guise of generalizations about the French. They may say you can't generalize and then go on to make generalizations that they firmly believe.

A Larousse publication, *Francoscopie*, summarizes hundreds of sociological studies and opinion polls in order to present a composite portrait of the French. One of the ideas behind *Francoscopie* is that French attitudes dictate lifestyle choices. France is compared to other countries and groups of the French are compared to other groups of the French.

If I wanted to know why someone was anti-American I wouldn't ask, *Pourquoi détestez-vous les Américains?* because the person would be sure to protest. *Mais non! Ce n'est pas ça!* Rather, I would say *Qu'est-ce que les Français reprochent aux Américains?* "What do the French criticize Americans for?" And that way I'd probably find out by the end of the conversation what the person thought. A French friend once said to me, *Les Américains n'aiment pas généraliser*, "Americans don't like to generalize." The French do not seem to be as wary of rather large generalizations, as long as these are not taken as stereotypes. They also seem to me to be more willing to debate questions to which there's no correct answer. But that's a generalization!

TOP TEN Questions Calling for Generalizations About the French

1. **Quel est le point fort des Français?** What is the strong point of the French?

2. **Les Français aiment-ils les grosses voitures?** Do the French like big cars?

3. **Les Français aiment-ils les chats?** Do the French like cats? (See the movie *Chacun cherche son chat*, *When the Cat's Away*.)

4. **Les Français passent-ils trop de temps devant la télé?** Do the French spend too much time in front of the TV set?

5. **Quelle émission préfèrent les Français et pourquoi?** What TV program do the French like best and why?

6. **De quoi les Français ont-ils besoin pour être heureux?** What do the French need in order to be happy?

7. **Que pensent les Français de la peine de mort?** What do the French think about the death penalty?

8. **Les Français aiment-ils faire la cuisine?** Do the French like to cook?

9. **Quelle est la plus grande différence entre la mentalité française et la mentalité américaine à votre avis?** What's the biggest difference between the French mentality and the American in your opinion?

10. **Est-il plus difficile pour un Français que pour un autre de quitter son pays pour vivre ailleurs avec quelqu'un dont il serait amoureux?** Is it more difficult for a French person than for someone who's not French to leave his country to live somewhere else with someone he's in love with?

Le plus beau village de France

The French are, on the whole, knowledgeable about France. If they don't know a fact about France today, they'll probably want to find it out for you by tomorrow. They are also willing to talk about aesthetic preferences and about the comparative merits of places that can't be ranked.

One hundred forty-six French villages throughout France are classified as *les plus beaux villages de France*. In practice, being collectively *les plus beaux villages* means that each of the villages has the right to be called *le plus beau village de France*, meaning not that it's the most beautiful village in France but that it has been officially classified.

When you call something *le plus beau* making a subjective and therefore subjunctive judgement, you say, *C'est le plus beau village que je connaisse*. If you are talking about something that can be measured objectively—for example, the height of a building—you'd say *C'est le plus haut bâtiment que je connais*. In this special case the villages seem to have met objective criteria for being *le plus beau*.

TOP TEN Questions About France

1. **Quel est le plus beau paysage de la France à votre avis?** What's the most beautiful landscape in France, in your opinion?

2. **Dans quelle ville française vit-on le mieux?** Which French city is the best to live in?

3. **Quelle est la plus belle cathédrale française à votre avis?** What's the most beautiful French cathedral, in your opinion?

4. **Quelle est l'importance de l'artisanat en France?** What's the importance of craftsmanship in France?

5. **L'artisanat est-il en train de disparaître en France?** Are artisans (and the tradition of craftsmanship) disappearing in France?

6. **Pourriez-vous expliquer le succès de la BD pour adultes en France?** Could you explain the success of comics for adults in France? (*la bande dessinée*)

7. **Qu'est-ce qui marche bien en France à votre avis?** What's successful in France, in your opinion?

8. **Quels progrès restent à faire en France?** What still needs improvement in France?

9. **Les Français élèvent-ils bien leurs enfants?** Do the French raise their children well?

10. **Quelles sont les fêtes françaises les plus importantes?** What are the most important French holidays?

Le carnet

If you ask an interesting question, someone will always want to answer it. Have a small notebook handy so that you can write down new expressions as soon as possible after the conversation.

Un cahier and *un carnet* are both notebooks. *Un cahier* is more apt to be the notebook used in school as an exercise book. *Un carnet* could be *un carnet d'adresses*, "an address book" or *un carnet de tickets de métro*. But *un carnet* is also the kind of notebook writers take notes in. Some of the scenes in Albert Camus's novels came directly from observations that Camus made in his *carnets*. *Un journal* is a journal or diary, as well as being a newspaper.

Here are some examples of the kind of questions that you might want to ask about French terms.

TOP TEN Questions About French Symbols, Concepts, and Controversies

1. **Que pensez-vous de la pyramide du Louvre?** What do you think of the Louvre pyramid?

2. **Comment trouvez-vous la TGB?** What do you think of the national library? (*TGB = la très grande bibliothèque*)

3. **Auriez-vous aimé prendre le Concorde?** Would you have liked to take the Concorde? (Followed by *Pourquoi?* or *Pourquoi pas?*)

4. **Quelles sont les meilleures lignes du TGV à votre avis?** What are the best routes of the fast train in your opinion? (*TGV* = *le train à grande vitesse*)

5. **Qu'est-ce que** *la laïcité?* What is secularism?

6. **Qu'est-ce que** *la malbouffe?* What is *la malbouffe?* (from *mal*, "badly," and *la bouffe*, slang for "food or eating")

7. **Les Français sont-ils je-m'en-foutistes?** Do the French have a couldn't-care-less attitude?

8. **Que veut dire** *bleu blanc beur?* What does *bleu blanc beur* mean? (See the *verlan* section of slang repair in Tune-Up 7.)

9. **Qu'est-ce que** *la France profonde?* What's "real France"? (literally, deep France)

10. **Expliquez le système D, s'il vous plaît.** Explain the *système D*, please. (*D* = *se débrouiller*)

La conversation et la discussion

Perhaps *la conversation* is a more American form of discourse than *la discussion* if, as the French claim, Americans like agreement and happy endings. In French there's a nuance of meaning missing in English according to which *une conversation* is relatively tame while *une discussion* can be a raging debate. *Discuter* has the same meaning as *se disputer* in the West African francophone countries such as Senegal and Ivory Coast. In France it often does too. A conversation can be either lively or subdued, but in any case the norm is for people to say politely whatever they really think or remain silent.

In *une discussion*, argument can be enjoyed for its own sake. It's almost expected that friends will take opposite sides of *une discussion* as though they were trying to win debating points. Actually just about any *conversation* topic can become a *discussion* topic. And a *discussion* topic is usually turned around until it becomes a controversy. Arguing with your friends and even interrupting them in this context is a sign of friendship rather than of hostility, and it's rare for any animosity to linger after a good *discussion*. Sometimes *la discussion* follows the form of the French essay, *la dissertation*, with a thesis, antithesis, and finally a synthesis that combines the different points harmoniously. That doesn't necessarily happen.

TOP TEN Questions to Ask to Start a Conversation

1. **Qu'est-ce que les Français admirent le plus chez les Américains?** What do the French admire the most in Americans?

2. **Peut-on bien manger aux Etats-Unis à votre avis?** Can you eat well in the United States in your opinion?

3. **Mange-t-on aussi bien à New York qu'à Paris?** Is the food as good in New York as in Paris?

4. **Y a-t-il de bons vins américains à votre avis?** Are there any good American wines in your opinion?

5. **Quels auteurs américains aime-t-on lire en France?** What American writers are popular in France?

6. **Combien de semaines de vacances ont les Français?** How many weeks of vacation do the French have?

7. **Combien d'heures a la semaine de travail en France maintenant?** How many hours does the French workweek have now?

8. **Avez-vous des traditions familiales?** Do you have family traditions?

9. **Pourquoi les Français ne font-ils pas autant de jogging que les Américains à votre avis?** Why do the French not do as much jogging as Americans, in your opinion?

10. **Préférez-vous les films américains ou français?** Do you prefer American films or French ones?

TOP TEN Questions to Ask to Start a Discussion

1. **Comment trouvez-vous le système des élections—aux Etats-Unis et en France?** How do you find the system of elections in the United States and in France?

2. **Pourriez-vous expliquer le deuxième tour des élections françaises?** Could you explain the second round of French elections?

3. **Que pensez-vous de la loi sur la parité?** What do you think of the parity law? (According to which an equal number of male and female candidates must initially be candidates for election.)

4. **Quelle est l'attitude des Français envers le McDo?** What's the French attitude toward McDonald's?

5. **Doit-on pouvoir se servir d'un portable dans un restaurant?** Should one be able to use a cell phone in a restaurant?

6. **Y-a-t-il des vices bien français?** Are there any specifically French vices?

7. **Le franglais présente-t-il un danger réel pour le français?** Is "franglais" a real danger for the French language?

8. **Les Français trouvent-ils que les Américains sont puritains?** Do the French find Americans puritanical?

9. **Y a t-il du racisme en France?** Is there racism in France?

10. **Le tourisme est-il bon pour la France?** Is tourism good for France?

Rehearsal Time

Give the practical question for each of the following answers.

1. On peut facilement y aller à pied ou bien vous pouvez y aller à vélo si vous préférez.

2. Il faut à peu près vingt minutes pour y aller.

3. Vous devez descendre à Saint-Germain-des-Prés. (a metro stop)

4. Non, c'est tout près.

5. Vous pouvez la garer devant la maison, par là.

Suggest the appropriate personal question for each of the following answers:

6. Je suis parisienne.

7. Je suis célibataire.

8. Je suis médecin.

9. C'est le 01.46.27.03.24.

10. C'est sophielebrun@wanadoo.fr.

11. C'est le 26 rue de Courcelles, 75016 Paris.

12. Je ne m'intéresse à aucun parti.

13. Non, je n'ai pas encore de projets.

14. Oui, vous pouvez m'accompagner si vous voulez.

15. Oui. Mes parents sont en vie tous les deux.

Here are some subjective answers to questions about France. What were the questions?

16. A mon avis, on vit le mieux à Grenoble.

17. Il y a beaucoup de très beaux paysages. Les Alpes, la côte de la Bretagne, la côte d'Azur, et la Dordogne sont très belles parmi d'autres, mais, selon moi, il est trop difficile de choisir le plus beau paysage.

18. Chartres est la plus belle cathédrale française, à mon avis.

19. En général, les Français élèvent bien leurs enfants parce que la famille est très importante pour les Français, mais il y a des exceptions bien sûr.

20. Les fêtes françaises les plus importantes pour beaucoup de Français sont Noël et le jour de l'an.

Now reverse the situation. Give your own "answers to the answers" using the questions for 6–20.

Slang and Other Kinds of French

Find the French That's Right for You

1. How do you say "slang" in French?

2. Why is the *tu* form more common than the *vous* form in slang?

3. In Marseille, how do you say, "He's crazy"?

4. What is meant by *Ne lâchez pas la patate*, and where would you say it?

5. In Senegal, what is *une case*?

6. In Belgium, how do you say *quatre-vingt-dix*?

7. What has happened to someone if you hear that *Il s'est cassé la gueule*?

8. What is meant by *mon vieux* and *mes vieux*?

9. Which French president was known as *tonton*?

10. If you hear someone say, *Je vais chez le toubib*, whom is he going to see?

11. What is *le verlan*?

12. Explain what is meant by *laisse béton*.

13. How do you say "what's-his-name" in French?

14. What is meant by *C'est un crack*?

15. What are the meanings of *une vache*, *c'est vache*, *c'est une vache à lait*, and *vachement*?

16. How do teenagers use *à la limite*?

17. What are *les gros mots*, and which of them are the most treacherous for people whose first language is not French?

18. What are two different meanings of *merde*?

19. What's the difference between *pute* and *putain*?

20. How can you say in three words in familiar French *Où est-ce que tu vas*?

Spoken French involves all sorts of choices. How do you decide which French you should use? The French of France? Belgium? Senegal? Quebec? Haiti? The French of Paris? Marseille? Should your speech be formal? Informal? Slang? When is it appropriate to use business French? Scientific French? The French used in the arts? Where do you start? *Tune Up Your French* deals mostly with everyday conversational French as understood throughout France. It's important to recognize, though, that there is no single norm for French and that the language is constantly evolving.

There is no isolated French expression that you can point to and say, "This is what and how all French people think." Obviously, all of the various French-speaking people have a lot of different ideas and they say many different things. They all speak French, though, and once you know a wide variety of French expressions, your sense of what sounds French starts to kick in.

The French that's right for you depends on who and where you are. All sorts of codes relate to the various levels of French among which you'll learn to navigate. If you're a young woman living in Quebec City you'll need a different French from that of an old man living in Tahiti or of a businesswoman living in Abidjan. Standard French can vary from country to country. Within a country, French can vary by region, social class, profession, and among generations. French mothers complain that they have a hard time understanding their teenage children because of all the slang they use.

By its nature, slang is for insiders so be careful as you expand your range. French *argot*, slang, is wide-ranging and creative. Within French there are so many forms of slang that understanding the language can seem challenging even if you're French. Slang is so common that you need to learn to recognize and understand even the kinds of slang that you shouldn't use yourself. Also, if you're going to use slang, it helps not to take yourself too seriously.

The cartoons of Claire Brétécher provide excellent examples of slang, as do the songs of Georges Brassens and Renaud. These models will make you admire French slang and want to learn it.

Slang uses the *tu* form almost exclusively. Because slang is so informal, it's impossible to imagine someone saying *Votre gueule!* or *Fermez votre gueule!* instead of *Ferme ta gueule!* or *Ta gueule!* or *Ferme-la!*—the equivalents of "Shut up!"

Just as with other kinds of French, which slang you can use and which you can't depends on who and where you are. You speak a different way at fifteen than at fifty, at the disco and at the dinner table. It sounds funny when someone uses slang in a way that's not convincingly natural, or when someone uses the slang of another group. This can happen when a parent tries to fit in with the younger generation by using their slang. And it's even more of a problem if French is not your first language. Some adolescents thrive on having their own slang and changing it often enough to keep an edge.

Laissez les bons temps rouler

Within France, someone from Marseille might say *Il est fada* to mean "He's nuts" or "He's being stupid." Since French is spoken throughout the world, no one can expect to know all of the variations not only within France but also from country to country and continent to continent. Different kinds of French aren't necessarily slang. Here are some examples of variations on French from Europe, Africa, and North America.

In some countries the words for numbers are different. In Belgium you can talk about *septante*, "seventy," and *une septantaine*, "about seventy of something." Some vocabulary variations come from cultural differences. *Le griot*, "the storyteller," and *le grigri*, "the charm or magical object," are part of West African cultures. *Une case* is a traditional West African house, so it replaces *une maison* without being the same thing. In Quebec there are expressions like *un chum*, "friend," that come directly from English, while there's sometimes an attempt to avoid English at all costs—resulting in *un chien chaud* for what the French call *un hot dog*. Meals have different names in Quebec too, with the three daily meals being *le déjeuner*, *le dîner*, and *le souper*. This sort of transposition happens in Louisiana as well, where what the French call *l'harmonica* becomes *la musique à bouche* and *l'accordéon* is *la musique à bras*.

TOP TEN Examples of French Outside of France

1. **Il y en a septante.** (Belgium, Switzerland, Congo, Rwanda) (*Il y en a soixante-dix.*) There are seventy of them.

2. **Il y en a nonante.** (Belgium, Switzerland, Congo, Rwanda) (*Il y en a quatre-vingt-dix.*) There are ninety of them.

3. **Il y en a huitante.** (Switzerland) (*Il y en a quatre-vingts.*) There are eighty of them.

4. **Leur case se trouve à la campagne.** (Senegal) Their house is in the country.

5. **On écoute le griot.** (Senegal) They are listening to the griot (the storyteller, poet, singer).

6. **Il a un grigri.** (Senegal). He has a magical object.

7. **Ils vont au bazar pour acheter des provisions.** (Mauritania) They are going food shopping at the market.

8. **On peut l'acheter chez le dépanneur.** (Quebec) You can get it at the convenience store.

9. **Ne lâchez pas la patate.** (Quebec) (*Tenez bon.*) Don't give up.

10. **Laissez les bons temps rouler.** (Louisiana) Let the good times roll.

Le papier d'alu

French is full of abbreviations, so it's good to know them. An adult once asked me to pass him *le papier d'alu*, which sounded like *papié-dalu*. I was completely bewildered, not realizing that he was asking for *le papier d'aluminium*, "aluminum foil." What sounds sometimes like French baby talk to an American ear is used by people of all ages. People will speak not only about *les écolos* (*les écologistes*), but also *les prolos* (*les prolétariens*) and *les intellos* (*les intellectuels*). *Les produits bios*—*bios* for *biologiques*—are "organic produce."

The expression *métro, boulot, dodo* describes a worker's life comprised of taking the subway, going to work, and going to bed. *Métro* is an abbreviation for *le métropolitain*, *boulot* is slang for "work," and *dodo* is baby talk for *dormir*.

It's much more common to hear *le bus* and *le car* than *l'autobus* and *l'autocar*. *Le bus* is the bus that you take within a city and *le car* is the bus that goes between towns. The following French abbreviations are heard more often than their long forms.

TOP TEN Abbreviated Words

1. **On prend l'*apéro*.** (*apéritif*) We're having drinks before dinner.

2. **On va au *ciné*?** (*cinéma*) Want to go to the movies?

3. **C'est *extra*.** (*extraordinaire*) That's cool.

4. **C'est un *intello*.** (*un intellectuel*) He's an intellectual.

5. **Prends ton *imper*.** (*imperméable*) Bring your raincoat.

6. **Je vais prendre le *car*.** (*l'autocar*) I'm going to take the bus (to go to another town).

7. **Il est *sympa*.** (*sympathique*) He's nice.

8. **On va prendre le *métro*.** (*métropolitain*) We're going to take the subway.

9. **Il y va à *vélo*.** (*vélocipède*) He's going there on his bike.

10. **Nous regardons la *télé* ce soir.** (*télévision*) We're watching TV tonight.

Elle est branchée

There are some slang expressions that *everyone* uses. Some, like *une gaffe*, are so completely acceptable that they are hardly recognized as slang. One of the most flattering French compliments is to be called *branché* because it means you are "hip," "with it," "in the know." Being able to use basic slang makes you a bit more *branché*.

TOP TEN Examples of Slang That Everyone Uses

1. **Je suis sidéré(e).** I'm stupefied.

2. **J'ai un rencard.** (*J'ai un rendez-vous.*) I have a date.

3. **J'en ai marre.** I've had it.

4. **C'est un projet farfelu.** It's a hare-brained plan.

5. **Manque de pot!** No luck! Too bad!

6. **Elle est branchée.** She's in the know.

7. **C'est génial.** That's cool.

8. **Je dois bosser pour cet examen.** I have to work hard for that exam.

9. **C'est du charabia.** That's gibberish.

10. **Je dois garer ma bagnole.** I've got to park my car.

TOP TEN Examples of Slang That Almost Everyone Uses

1. **Voilà un flic.** There's a cop.

2. **Qu'est-ce que tu fabriques?** What are you doing?

3. **Je pige.** I get it.

4. **Elles aiment les fringues.** They like clothes.

5. **Ça gaze?** How's it going? What's up? The answer: **Ça gaze.**
   Great. Everything's going well.

6. **J'ai plein de boulot.** I've got plenty of work to do.

7. **On va bouffer.** We're going to go eat.

8. **Il/Elle est gonflé(e).** He/She is full of himself/herself.

9. **Je prends un verre de pinard.** I'll have a glass of wine.

10. **C'est pas mon truc.** It's not my thing.

 Examples of Slang That Hardly Anyone Finds Objectionable

1. **Tu as piqué un crayon?** Did you take (steal) a pencil?

2. **Je flippe.** I'm flipping out.

3. **Il est râleur.** He's in a bad mood. **Elle est râleuse.** She likes
   to complain.

4. **Elle a du culot.** She's got a nerve.

5. **On a bien rigolé.** We had a good laugh.

6. **Il s'est cassé la gueule.** He fell on his face.

7. **Ils s'engueulent toujours.** They are always fighting.

8. **Je craque.** I'm losing it.

9. **Ça flotte.** It's raining.

10. **On est fauché.** We're broke.

TOP TEN   Slang Appraisals

1. **C'est chouette.** It's cool.

2. **C'est nul.** It's no good.

3. **C'est moche.** It's ugly.

4. **C'est rigolo.** It's funny.

5. **C'est barbant.** It's boring.

6. **C'est ringard.** It's out of style.

7. **C'est dément.** It's nutty.

8. **C'est dingue.** It's weird.

9. **C'est vache.** It's mean.

10. **C'est au poil!** It's great!

Mon vieux

Salut, mon vieux is something a man might say to one of his male buddies: "Hi, pal." But if he refers to someone as *mon vieux*, he's talking about his father. *Tonton*, a word for "uncle," was also the nickname of François Mitterand. DeGaulle's wife, who always stayed discreetly in the background, used to be called *la tante Yvonne*.

You can use most slang and informal expressions for various relatives and acquaintances without causing a stir. Some of these expressions, however, can be used in an ironic tone and carry a derogatory connotation, so it's better to avoid them unless you're either completely fluent in French or in the company of indulgent friends. The phrases with an asterisk (*) in the following list are questionable.

TOP TEN Ways to Introduce Family Members in Slang

1. **Ce sont mon vieux et ma vieille.*** (*papa et maman*) That's Ma and Pa. (Mom and Dad)

2. **Voilà mes vieux.*** Those are my parents, the old folks.

3. **Voilà mon frangin et ma frangine.** There's my brother and sister.

4. **Ce sont mes gosses.** These are my kids.

5. **C'est Pépé et Mémé.** There's Granny and Granddad.

6. **C'est ma tatie.** There's my auntie. Also, *tata*.

7. **C'est mon tonton.** That's my uncle.

8. **C'est mon beauf.** That's my brother-in-law.

9. **C'est mon beau-dab et ma belle-doche.*** That's my father-in-law and my mother-in-law.

10. **Et leur fiston et leur fifille.*** And their son and daughter.

Copain, copine

As in English, talking about one's "significant other" in French is a tricky business. Talking about *mon petit ami* and *ma petite amie* is very clear, but it sounds childish after age twenty-five.

You can have *un grand ami* and *une grande amie*, but these people are great friends. *Mon copain* and *ma copine* in the singular can refer to a boyfriend and a girlfriend, respectively. *C'est un copain* means just "This is my friend," whereas *C'est mon copain* usually means "He's my boyfriend." To introduce a boyfriend or girlfriend, most people would say *C'est mon ami* and *C'est mon amie* along with the person's name. The meaning of boyfriend or girlfriend is usually clear enough from the context.

TOP TEN Other Folks, Including So-and-So

1. **C'est un gamin. C'est une gamine.** He/She is just a kid.

2. **C'est mon pote.** That's my buddy.

3. **Les nanas viennent de partir.** The women just left.

4. **Les mecs viennent d'arriver.** The guys just got here.

5. **Il/Elle amène Tartempion.** He's/She's bringing what's-his-name.

6. **Et ils ont présenté M. et Mme Untel.** And they introduced Mr. and Mrs. So-and-So.

7. **Je dois aller chez le toubib.** I've got to go see the doctor.

8. **Ce sont des copains.** These are some friends. (*Un copain* is a friend or a boyfriend. *Une copine* is a friend or a girlfriend.)

9. **C'est mon petit ami. C'est ma petite amie.** This is my boyfriend/girlfriend.

10. **C'est un crack.** He's a brain.

C'est vachement bien

Une vache, "a cow," lends herself to slang such as *Oh la vache!* "Wow!" *C'est vache!* "That's mean!" *C'est une vache à lait.* "That's a source of easy money" (literally, "a milk cow"). Exchange students come back from France speaking French much more fluently than when they left. They proudly use expressions like *vachement* in preference to *très* and *Je m'en fous* ("I don't give a damn") instead of the more sedate *Je m'en fiche*. *A la limite* is thrown into sentences where it doesn't mean anything, in accordance with adolescent usage. *A la limite* is the rough equivalent of "I suppose" and is used the same way as "I mean." *C'est canon* is the French equivalent of "It's awesome."

Unless you consider it progress to pick up the colloquial uses of "like," "I mean," and "awesome," it's better to go easy on words like *vachement* and *à la limite*. The young can get away with saying *Ça boume* but it's harder for older Americans not to sound silly using the slang of another generation. If you listen for nuance rather than assuming that everyone uses the same kind of language, you get a feeling for the kind of informal language that's acceptable and appropriate for you. The hidden rules for levels of informality can be complicated. Fortunately this is a subject that can be discussed openly, and the ensuing conversations are a way of making friends.

TOP TEN of the *argot des ados*

1. **C'est vachement bien.** It's awesome.

2. **C'est canon.** It's dynamite.

3. **C'est géant.** It's tremendous.

4. **C'est sensass.** That's sensational.

5. **C'est hypercool.** It's wicked cool.

6. **C'est nullos.** It's hopeless.

7. **C'est craignos.** It's worthless.

8. **Ça boume?** How's it going? **Ça boume.** It's going great.

9. **C'est carrément débile.** It's really pathetic.

10. **J'veux bien y aller à la limite.** I mean I'd kind of like to go.

Le verlan

Le verlan, similar to pig Latin, reverses the syllables of words. The process for the word *verlan* goes like this: *l'envers, l'en vers, vers l'en, verslen, verlan. Verlan* goes back to the fifteenth century. The contemporary singer Renaud had a hit song «*Laisse béton*» (for *laisse tomber*), and the filmmaker Claude Berri made a film *Les Ripoux* from *les pourris*, "the rotten, good for nothings." *Les Ripoux* refers to crooked cops.

Français becomes *céfran*, and even an English word used in French can go from *cool* to *looc. Verlan* often starts with slang. For example, *une cigarette* is *une clope* in slang and then becomes *une péclot* in *verlan*.

Flic has been reversed a second time in *verlan*, but without going back to *flic. Agent de police* became *flic*, which became *keuf* in *verlan*, which then became *feuk*, in *reverlan* for insiders. *Keuf* had become too well known, and *feuk*, the second *verlan* version, was meant to sound like "fuck."

When France won the World Cup, everyone talked about *bleu, blanc, beur* instead of *bleu, blanc, rouge*, the colors of *le tricolore*, the French flag. The French soccer team proudly reflected the diversity of modern France, and the slogan also reflected the widespread understanding of *beur, arabe*, in *verlan*.

TOP TEN Things to Say in *verlan*

1. **Laisse *béton*.** (*Laisse tomber.*) Drop it.

2. **Demande à la *meuf*.** (*femme*) Ask the woman.

3. **Y avait un *keum*.** (*mec*) There was a guy there.

4. **Gare au *keuf*.** (*flic*) Watch out for the cop.

5. **C'est des *Beurs*.** (*Arabes*) They're second-generation North Africans.

6. **Je prends un *féca*.** (*café*) I'm having a coffee.

7. **T'as vu le film, *Les Ripoux*?** (*pourris*) Did you see the movie, *Les Ripoux*?

8. **Il est *chébran*.** (*branché*) He's plugged in. He's in the know.

9. ***Malva*.** (*Ça va mal.*) Things are going badly.

10. ***Patouche*.** (*Ne touche pas!*) Don't touch!

«*Putain, putain, putain*»

There's some slang you should be particularly wary of, even if it seems as if everyone else uses it casually. The literal meanings of these words are crude even though they don't attract much attention until someone who is not French uses them. These words have at least two meanings according to how the words sound when the French say them and how they sound when you say them. This phenomenon exists in any language, of course.

One of the questions that Bernard Pivot had to answer on the last episode of his TV show, "Apostrophes," was *Quel est votre juron, gros mot ou blasphème favori?* which means "What's your favorite curse word?" Pivot's answer was «*Putain, trois fois. Putain, putain, putain.*»

Putain! has the effect of "Damn!" from the French, but it literally means "whore" and it may suddenly sound like "Whore!" from you. *Putain* is often used just to mean "Too bad! Bad luck!" It's used so often as a swear that it's not used to mean "whore" anymore. That has changed to *une pute*.

Tu déconnes sounds like "That's a stupid thing to say!" from the French. They would hear "You're fucking up!" if you said it. *Salaud!* is "Jerk!" when they say it, and "Bastard!" if you say it. Just the fact of using these words at all can seem disrespectful. On the other hand, it can sound funny.

Within France there are many kinds of slang for different groups, but some slang expressions have become more common than standard French throughout France. Most of the French can understand and speak more or less the same standard spoken French (bourgeois Parisian French) when they want to, and this prescribed

French is the French that they usually expect you to speak if you're not French. Slang is the badge of the in-group.

TOP TEN Slang Phrases That You Should Not Say in Polite Company

1. **Tu me fais chier.** You're getting on my nerves. (Literally, you're making me shit.)

2. **Vous vous foutez de moi?** Are you making fun of me? Are you fucking with me?

3. **Faut que j'aille aux chiottes.** I have to go to the bathroom. (derivative of *chier*, "to shit")

4. **C'est chiant.** It's boring. It's annoying. (literally, shitty)

5. **Putain!** Damn it! (literally, whore)

6. **Fous-moi la paix.** Leave me alone. Leave me the fuck alone.

7. **Ferme ta gueule.** Be quiet. Shut your trap.

8. **Fous le camp.** Go away. Fuck off.

9. **C'est le bordel.** What a mess. (literally, whorehouse)

10. **Je m'en fous.** I don't give a damn.

Les gros mots

Les gros mots, as seen above and below, are "swears." Variations of *con* ("idiot") and *merde* ("darn"/"shit") are particularly treacherous. They are often considered natural and pass unnoticed among refined, well-educated people, but don't kid yourself that you'll sound authentic and unobtrusive using *des gros mots*.

Merde! sounds like "Darn!" when they say it, like "Shit!" when you say it. *Merde!* has another meaning, too. You can say it to an actor before a play meaning "Good luck! Break a leg!"

TOP TEN Members of the *merde* and *con* families

1. **Merde!** If they say it = "Oh no!" If you say it = "Shit!"

2. **Tu m'emmerdes.** If they say it = "Cut it out." If you say it = "You're full of shit."

3. **C'est emmerdant.** If they say it = "It's a bore." If you say it = "It's a pain in the ass."

4. **Je suis dans la merde.** If they say it = "I've got a problem." If you say it = "I'm in deep shit."

5. **Je veux bien mais il y a des emmerdements.** If they say it = "I'd like to but I've got some annoying things to do that are creating a problem." If you say it = "I'd like to but there's some shit I have to take care of."

6. **Essaie de te démerder pour venir.** If they say it = "Try to get out of those commitments so you can come." If you say it = "Try to get out of doing that shit."

7. **C'est con.** If they say it = "That's dumb." If you say it = "That's a bitch."

8. **Ils sont cons. Elles sont connes.** If they say it = "They're jerks." If you say it = "They're stupid assholes."

9. **Tu déconnes.** If they say it = "You're not making sense. You don't know what you're talking about." If you say it = "You're bullshitting."

10. **Il est un peu connard. Elle est un peu connarde.** If they say it = "He/She is a bit out of it." If you say it = "He/She is a bit of an asshole."

Regarde-moi ça!

Not only are vocabulary and idioms different in familiar French, but so are some grammatical constructions. An *e* can be unpronounced as in *J'veux bien* or *J'suis crevé*. An extra word can be added so that *Regarde ça!* becomes *Regarde-moi ça*. The negative *ne* is dropped in expressions like *T'en as pas?* or *Touche pas*. In the expression *il y a*, the *il* can be dropped as in *Y en a plus* or *Y a personne*. *Veux-tu* becomes *Tu veux?* Sentences are broken up for emphasis, as in *J'ai rien dit, moi* or *Ton match, c'était plutôt débile*. *A qui* and *à quoi* can move to the end of a sentence and there's no inversion: *Tu penses à quoi?* Words like *quand* and *pourquoi* can move to the end of the sentence, too. Sometimes with *est-ce que* the *est-ce* is dropped but the *que* part stays in a sentence, giving *Pourquoi qu'y dit ça?* Finally, the future is rarely used with slang. You can say, *Je viens demain*. The following list summarizes these ten idiosyncrasies.

TOP TEN Colloquial Constructions

1. **J'suis crevé.** (*Je suis fatigué.*) I'm dead tired. (unpronounced *e*)

2. **Regarde-moi ça.** (*Regarde!*) Take a look at that. (extra words)

3. **Touche pas.** (*Ne touche pas.*) Don't touch. (The negative form *ne* has been dropped.)

4. **Y a personne.** (*Il n'y a personne.*) There's no one there. (The *Il* and *n'* of *Il n'y a personne* have been dropped.)

5. **Tu veux parler à qui?** (*A qui veux-tu parler?*) Who would you like to speak to? (*A qui* was moved to the end of the sentence and there's no inversion.)

6. **Ton match, c'était plutôt débile.** (*Ton match n'était pas impressionnant.*) Your game was pretty pathetic. (The sentence was segmented for emphasis.)

7. **Tu pars quand?** (*Quand est-ce que tu pars?*) When are you going to leave? (*Quand* goes to the end of the sentence. The

same thing can happen with *pourquoi, combien, comment*, and *où*.)

8. **Pourquoi tu n'es pas venu?** (*Pourquoi n'es-tu pas venu?*) Why didn't you come? (The inversion is dropped after *pourquoi*. This can happen with *combien, comment, quand,* and *où* as well.)

9. **Pourquoi qu'y dit ça?** (*Pourquoi est-ce qu'il dit ça?*) Why does he say that? (The *est-ce* of *est-ce que* has been dropped.)

10. **Il revient dans une heure.** (*Il reviendra dans une heure.*) He'll be back in an hour. (The present tense is used in place of the future.)

Où tu vas?

When people are in a hurry, they speak in shorthand. Just as words become abbreviated, questions in slang become shorter. Some of the most common questions in familiar French sound like a single word. They have become *formules figées*, "fixed expressions."

TOP TEN Abbreviated Questions

1. **Où tu vas?** (*Où est-ce que tu vas?*) Where're you going?

2. **Pourquoi t'as dit ça?** (*Pourquoi as-tu dit ça?*) Why'd you say that?

3. **A quand les vacances?** (*Quand aurons-nous des vacances?*) When are we going to get a vacation?

4. **T'as fait quoi?** (*Qu'est-ce que tu as fait?*) What'd you do?

5. **C'est quand?** (*Quand est-ce que c'est?*) When is it?

6. **Qui c'est qui a dit ça?** (*Qui est-ce qui a dit cela?*) Who said that?

7. **Tu l'vois comment?** (*Comment le vois-tu?*) How d'you see it?

8. **Pourquoi t'as rien dit?** (*Pourquoi n'as-tu rien dit?*) How come you didn't say anything?

9. **T'as pas de fric?** (*N'as-tu pas d'argent?*) Don't you have any cash?

10. **Combien t'en as?** (*Combien est-ce que tu en as?*) How much/many do you have?

Rehearsal Time

Choose the expression that best corresponds to the given slang expression:

1. J'ai un rencard.
   a. J'ai un rendez-vous.
   b. J'ai un brancard.
   c. Je suis en retard.

2. J'en ai marre.
   a. C'est marrant.
   b. Je suis excédé.
   c. Je suis heureux.

3. Manque de pot!
   a. Rien à boire.
   b. Pas de chance.
   c. J'ai raté le pot.

4. Il est branché.
   a. Il se perche sur une branche.
   b. Il est toujours au courant.
   c. Il ne sait pas ce qui se passe.

5. On amène les gosses?
   a. On amène les enfants?
   b. On amène les hommes?
   c. On cherche les animaux?

6. Voilà un flic.
   a. C'est un film excellent!
   b. Ça se passe en un clin d'œil.
   c. Voilà un agent.

7. Qu'est-ce que tu fabriques?
   a. Quel tissu choisis-tu pour cette robe?
   b. Qu'est-ce que tu fais?
   c. Vas-tu à l'usine?

8. Elles aiment les fringues.
   a. Elles aiment les vêtements.
   b. Elles sont marginales.
   c. Elles prennent des risques.

9. Ça gaze?
   a. Y a t-il assez d'essence?
   b. Vous y mettez du tigre?
   c. Ça va?

10. J'ai plein de boulot.
    a. J'ai grand appétit.
    b. J'ai beaucoup de travail.
    c. J'ai rempli mon verre.

11. On va bouffer.
    a. Nous allons manger.
    b. Nous allons mentir.
    c. Nous allons éclater de rire.

12. Il est râleur.
    a. Il se plaint toujours.
    b. C'est un grand chanteur.
    c. Il n'est jamais à l'heure.

13. C'est craignos.
    a. J'ai peur.
    b. C'est mauvais!
    c. C'est excellent!

14. Ça flotte.
    a. C'est du savon.
    b. Ça se comprend facilement.
    c. Il pleut.

15. On est fauché.
    a. On est riche.
    b. On est épuisé.
    c. On n'a pas d'argent.

16. C'est moche.
    a. C'est mou.
    b. C'est laid.
    c. C'est artistique.

17. C'est barbant.
    a. C'est du fer barbelé.
    b. C'est piquant.
    c. C'est ennuyeux.

18. C'est ringard.
    a. C'est exact.
    b. C'est démodé.
    c. Ça ne tourne pas rond.

19. C'est au poil!
    a. Tu devrais te raser les jambes!
    b. C'est super!
    c. Tout le monde sera nu!

20. C'est Tonton.
    a. C'est mon oncle.
    b. C'est mon chien.
    c. C'est tout ce qu'il y a de mieux.

8

Attitude

Use French Images to See Life the French Way

Preview

1. What's meant by *le mot juste*?

2. What's the difference between *l'esprit de l'escalier* and *l'esprit de la repartie*?

3. What French expression means that you take off an extra day between a holiday and a weekend?

4. What is meant by *le juste milieu*?

5. What English expressions do you know that use the French word *coup*?

6. What's the difference between *un coup de main* in English and *un coup de main* in French?

7. Give two examples of French expressions related to politics that are used in English.

8. What is meant by *un idiot savant*?

9. What kind of power is wielded by *une éminence grise*?

10. What are *les frites* and *le pain perdu* in English, and who took them off the menu at the House of Representatives?

11. Explain *Ils se sont roulé un patin.*

12. What does it mean if a French person says to you, *Vous parlez américain*?

13. What's the significance of the expression, *une araignée au plafond*?

14. What's the difference between being called *une peau de vache* and *une poule mouillée*?

15. Describe the activity known as *le trou normand*.

16. What can result in *la gueule de bois*?

17. What is meant by the expression *un ange passe*?

18. What's the real meaning of the title of Truffaut's film *Les 400 Coups*?

19. In what sort of situation would you say *J'ai d'autres chats à fouetter*?

20. What's the French equivalent of "He loves me, he loves me not" or "She loves me, she loves me not" when pulling off the petals of a daisy?

When you speak French you look at life the French way. The English idiom "We don't speak the same language" has an equivalent in French: *Nous ne parlons pas la même langue*, "We don't see things the same way." On the other hand, just by speaking the same language, you start to see things the way other people do.

When French has just the expression you need the French have a word for that too: *le mot juste*. For this reason, a French expression sometimes becomes adopted in English. The expression *un enfant terrible* fills a need in English. And sure enough, the Robert & Collins says that *un enfant terrible* is, in the figurative sense, "an enfant terrible." *Un enfant terrible* is usually a likable adult who shocks and amuses by controversially frank comments, regardless of the social consequences.

French also has words for ideas that you recognize but may not have been aware of because you didn't have words for them. Everyone has had experiences that would fit the expression *l'esprit de l'escalier*, "staircase wit." If you have *l'esprit de l'escalier* it means that you think of just the right rejoinder when it's too late, when you're leaving, going down the stairs after the party. This tune-up will help you make the transition from *l'esprit de l'escalier* to *l'esprit de la repartie*. That's when you think of the right thing to say at just the right moment.

On fait le pont

Making a bridge is the French tradition of making a one-day holiday into a four-day vacation. Many Americans would like to emulate the French custom of recognizing *le pont*, "the bridge," which links a holiday to a weekend so that they get at least four days off in a row.

Having *un embarras de richesses* means that too many good things are happening at the same time. If it's a problem, it's a good one to have. *Vous n'avez que l'embarras du choix* means "the only problem is how to decide."

Henri Bergson, a great French philosopher, argued that positive change is possible and that *l'élan vital*, "the creative force," makes it possible to change for the better. *L'art de vivre* means "the way of life," in much the same way that *le mode de vie* means "the lifestyle." *L'art de vivre* suggests nonetheless the concept that living is an art to be enjoyed.

TOP TEN Most Appreciated French Concepts

1. **Nous allons faire le pont.** We'll take [Friday] off too because we have [Thursday] off. (literally, do the bridge)

2. **Nous avons un embarras de richesses.** We have almost too much of a good thing. (literally, a problem of riches)

3. **On vous laisse carte blanche.** You have carte blanche. You can do whatever you like. (literally, white card)

4. **Nous voulons suivre une politique de détente.** We want to follow a strategy of détente among nations. (literally, the relaxation of tensions)

5. **C'est le juste milieu.** It's the happy medium. (literally, the right middle)

6. **Nous avons beaucoup de joie de vivre.** We have lots of joie de vivre. (joy of living)

7. **C'est un bain de jouvence.** It makes you feel young. (It's a bath from the fabled Jouvence fountain said to bring back youth.)

8. **Ils ont l'esprit de corps.** They have esprit de corps, loyalty, and team spirit. (literally, spirit of the body)

9. **C'est l'élan vital.** It's the creative force. (literally, the vital force)

10. **C'est l'art de vivre.** It's the way of life. (literally, the art of living)

Beau coup

Many French concepts, including some of those above, have been adopted unchanged by the English language. Often an artful combination of words creates a nuance missing in English. The combinations formed by *entente + cordiale, cause + célèbre, éminence + grise*, and *idiot + savant* create meanings that don't exist in English.

   The word *coup* gives rise to a number of idioms in English. There are over 150 idioms with *coup* in French. Among those that have made their way into English are: *un coup de grâce*, "a death blow"; *un coup de maître*, "a master blow"; *un coup d'Etat*, "an overthrow"; *un coup de théâtre*, "a dramatic turn of events"; and *un coup de main*, "a sudden attack." Usually these expressions have the same meaning in English as in French, but in French *un coup de main* is "a helping hand," whereas in English it's "a sudden attack." *Je voudrais vous donner un coup de main* means "I'd like to help you," not attack you.

TOP TEN Adopted Concepts

1. **Elle fait partie de l'avant-garde.** She's in the avant-garde, in the vanguard. (literally, ahead of guard)

2. **Ils ont une entente cordiale.** They have an entente cordiale, a good working relationship. (literally, cordial understanding)

3. **C'est sa raison d'être.** It's his/her raison d'être, justification for existence. (his/her reason to be)

4. **Ils sont toujours au courant.** They always are au courant, up-to-date with what's going on. (literally, in the current)

5. **C'est de rigueur.** It's de rigueur, the done thing, the accepted way. (of strict importance)

6. **C'est un fait accompli.** It's a fait accompli, already done, too late to change. (an accomplished fact)

7. **C'est une cause célèbre.** It's a cause célèbre, a topic of controversy. (literally, a famous cause)

8. **Ils ont fait un coup d'Etat.** They made a coup d'état, overthrew the government. (literally, blow of state)

9. **Lui, c'est un idiot savant.** He's an idiot savant, someone who although mentally defective is brilliant in one particular way. (literally, scholarly idiot)

10. **C'est une éminence grise.** He/She is an éminence grise. He/She is the power behind the throne. (literally, gray eminence)

Le pain perdu

French writers, journalists, and professors, most notably René Etiemble, a Sorbonne professor, have protested indignantly about *le franglais*, English words like *le blush-on* and *le hamburger* that are infiltrating French. American humorists and columnists such as Art Buchwald and Ellen Goodman wrote rejoinders about the American use of French words. Greeting the challenge, Goodman wrote: "If they make it *de rigueur* to eliminate Americanisms, we shall refuse to eat our apple pie *à la mode* and our *soupe du jour*. We shall, in fact, hoist them on their own petulant *pétard*."

French words such as *détente* and *carte blanche* had made their way into English without much ado. The same was true for English expressions with "French" in them, such as "French toast" and "French fries." Then in March 2003, Bob Ney and Walter Jones of the House of Representatives held a press conference to announce that three cafeterias in the office buildings of the American House of Representatives had changed their menus to replace French fries with "freedom fries" and French toast with "freedom toast."

In French, French fries are not "French." *Les frites* are associated with Belgium, and the closest thing to French toast is *le pain perdu* (literally, lost bread). Taking French leave is associated with the English: *On file à l'anglaise.*

TOP TEN Things That Are Called "French"

1. **Je vais acheter une *baguette*.** I'm going to buy some French bread.

2. **Ils ont une *porte-fenêtre* qui donne sur le jardin.** They have a French door that looks out on the garden.

3. **Elle fait une très bonne *vinaigrette* pour la salade.** She makes a very good French dressing for the salad.

4. **Il aime bien un steak *frites*.** He likes having a steak with French fries.

5. **Dans l'orchestre il joue du *cor d'harmonie*.** He plays the French horn in the orchestra.

6. **Ils se sont roulé un *patin*.** They French-kissed. (*Le patin* is slang for "the tongue.")

7. **Je vais filer *à l'anglaise*.** I'm going to take French leave.

8. **Dans son jardin il y a des *œillets d'Inde*.** In his/her garden, there are some French marigolds.

9. **Elle raffole du *pain perdu*.** She's crazy about French toast.

10. **Ils passent les vacances sur *la côte d'Azur*.** They're spending their vacation on the French Riviera.

On parle américain

Americans say we speak English, while the French say Americans speak *américain*, a different language from English. A translation of an American book into French will have been *traduit de l'américain*.

In a review of the French movie *Le Pacte des loups*, a *Boston Globe* reviewer, Ed Siegel, wrote that it was "a bit too French." One could guess what he meant, but would one say that any American movie was "a bit too American"? Consider the expressions that to Americans seem "very French." To the French, after all, these expressions don't seem particularly French. It takes two languages and two cultures to set each other in relief—often comic relief.

Revenons à nos moutons

Revenons à nos moutons means "Let's get back to the subject." In French, as in English, many metaphors and comparisons involve animals. *C'est la brebis galeuse de la famille* means that someone is the black sheep of the family. *C'est le bouc émissaire* means that someone is the scapegoat.

French doesn't always choose the same animal metaphors as English. Another term for a scapegoat is *le dindon de la farce*, literally, the turkey in the farce. If something is never going to happen you'd say, *Quand les poules auront des dents*, "When pigs fly." Animal metaphors also appear in other parts of this chapter: *une peau de vache, une poule mouillée, un chat dans la gorge*, and *J'ai d'autres chats à fouetter*. In the following list, compare the use of animal metaphors in French and in English.

TOP TEN Animal Metaphors

1. **Il/Elle a une araignée au plafond.** He/She has bats in the belfry. (literally, a spider on the ceiling)

2. **Il est heureux comme un poisson dans l'eau. Elle est heureuse comme un poisson dans l'eau.** He/She is as happy as a clam at high tide. (literally, as a fish in water)

3. **Il y a anguille sous roche.** I smell a rat. (Literally, there's an eel under the rock.)

4. **Il faut ménager la chèvre et le chou.** You have to run with the hare and hunt with the hounds. (Literally, you have to han-

dle the goat and the cabbage tactfully; the idea is to keep the goat from eating the cabbage.)

5. **On le/la jette dans la fosse aux lions.** He/She is being thrown to the wolves. (literally, into the lion's pit)

6. **Il/Elle se jette dans la gueule du loup.** He/She is putting his/her hand in the lion's mouth. (literally, into the wolf's mouth)

7. **Il/Elle court deux lièvres à la fois.** He/She is riding two horses at the same time. (literally, racing two hares)

8. **Il/Elle met la charrue avant les boeufs.** He/She is putting the cart before the horse. (literally, the plow in front of the oxen)

9. **Ce n'est pas à un vieux singe qu'on apprend à faire des grimaces.** You can't teach an old dog new tricks. (Literally, you can't teach an old monkey to make faces.)

10. **Elle a du chien.** She's foxy. She's attractive. (Literally, she has some of the dog.)

Les casse-pieds

There's a whole repertoire of expressions in any language for describing annoying people. Some French expressions such as *Il me casse les pieds*, *Elle me casse les pieds* along with their epithets such as *Il est casse-pieds*, *Elle est casse-pieds* are heard constantly. Others such as *C'est une peau de vache* are heard less often, perhaps because they are reserved for the biggest jerks. Either a man or a woman can be *une peau de vache*.

Un arriviste is unscrupulous and wants to get ahead at all costs. *Il se comporte en nouveau riche* means he's ostentatious (and acts like *un nouveau riche*). French preppies are *BCBG, Bon chic, bon genre* or

FHCP, foulard Hermès collier de perles. The stereotype is someone wearing a Hermès scarf and a pearl necklace.

There aren't as many colorful images for nice people. You usually hear them described simply as *bien* or *sympa.* You say *Il est bien* or *Elle est bien.*

TOP TEN French Ways to Describe Jerks

1. **C'est une peau de vache.** He's a nasty bastard. She's a bitch. He/She is a skunk. (literally, cowhide)

2. **Elle est venue comme un cheveu sur la soupe.** She arrived at just the wrong moment. (like a hair in soup)

3. **C'est un/une trouble-fête.** He/She is a spoilsport. (party pooper)

4. **Il est imbuvable, celui-là.** I can't stand him. (literally, he's undrinkable)

5. **Il est casse-pieds.** He gets on my nerves. He's a pain in the neck. (literally, foot breaker)

6. **C'est une mauvaise langue.** He/She is a nasty gossip. (literally, a bad tongue)

7. **C'est une poule mouillée.** He/She is a wimp, a scaredy-cat. (literally, a wet chicken)

8. **Il se croit le moutardier du pape.** He thinks he's hot stuff. (literally, the pope's mustard maker)

9. **C'est un pauvre type.** He/She is pathetic. (literally, a poor type)

10. **Lui/Elle, c'est ma bête noire.** He/She is the most annoying person. **Ça, c'est ma bête noire.** That's what I hate most, my pet peeve. (literally, a black beast)

Un ange passe

French metaphors have a way of getting our attention and providing enough distance to let us see a situation with irony. *Ça met du beurre dans les épinards* is a compelling description of a way to improve a situation. Alluding to a pause in conversation by saying that *un ange passe* can ease an awkward silence in a conversation. Knowing the metaphor *le trou normand*—an expression referring to a custom that we may have no apparent use for and probably would not wish to emulate—adds to the enjoyment of life.

TOP TEN French Metaphors

1. **Ça met du beurre dans les épinards.** That helps ease the finances. (literally, puts butter on the spinach)

2. **J'ai passé une nuit blanche.** I had a sleepless night. (literally, a white night)

3. **J'ai dormi sur les deux oreilles.** I slept soundly. (literally, on both ears)

4. **C'est une pierre dans mon jardin.** That's an insult. (literally, a stone in my garden)

5. **Il était entre chien et loup.** It was dusk. (literally, between dog and wolf)

6. **Il y perd son latin.** He doesn't know what to make of it. (literally, loses his Latin over it)

7. **Il y a une ombre au tableau.** There's a drawback. (literally, a shadow in the picture)

8. **Un ange passe.** There's an awkward silence. (literally, an angel passes)

9. **Elle a la gueule de bois.** She has a hangover. (literally, a wooden mouth)

10. **Si on faisait le trou normand.** Let's have a sip of Calvados (apple liqueur) between courses of the meal. (literally, the Norman hole)

J'ai d'autres chats à fouetter

The expression *J'ai d'autres chats à fouetter*, meaning "I have better things to do," has an undeniable kinkiness to it. Other French metaphors of action have lent themselves to the titles of novels and movies such as *Le Diable au corps* and *Les 400 Coups*. While Truffaut's movie *Les 400 Coups* is well known in the United States, the meaning of the title has often been unclear because of its mistranslation.

In each of the following expressions the figurative meaning is juxtaposed with the literal meaning of the expression.

TOP TEN Images of Mayhem

1. **Elle tire le diable par la queue.** She barely gets by. (literally, pulls the devil by its tail)

2. **Il est tombé dans les pommes.** He passed out. (literally, fell in the apples)

3. **Le torchon brûle.** Things are getting hot. There's a running battle going on. (Literally, the dish towel is burning.)

4. **C'est la danse macabre.** Death comes to people of all stations. (the allegorical *danse macabre* in which death, depicted as a dancing skeleton, comes to all)

5. **Ils ont mis des bâtons dans les roues.** They threw a monkey wrench into it. (literally, sticks in the wheels)

6. **Ils aiment enfoncer les portes ouvertes.** They like to go to a lot of trouble overcoming imaginary difficulties. (literally, break through open doors)

7. **Ils ont cassé du sucre sur son dos.** They spread malicious gossip about him/her in his/her absence. (literally, broke sugar on his/her back)

8. **J'ai d'autres chats à fouetter.** I have better things to do. I have other fish to fry. (literally, other cats to whip)

9. **Il a le diable au corps.** He's full of intense energy. He's overactive. (literally, has the devil in his body) *Le Diable au corps* is a novel by Raymond Radiguet and a movie by Claude Autant-Lara.

10. **Il a fait les 400 coups.** He sowed his wild oats. He led a disordered life. He painted the town red. (The English title of *Les 400 Coups* is *The 400 Blows*.)

TOP TEN Uncomfortable Positions

1. **On est dans le pétrin.** We're in a jam. (literally, the bread-kneading machine)

2. **Il se fait du mauvais sang.** He's worried. (Literally, he's making himself some bad blood.)

3. **Je me sens mal dans ma peau.** I feel ill at ease. (literally, bad in my skin)

4. **Je ne suis pas dans mon assiette.** I'm not feeling myself. (not in my seat, not at my place—which became "my plate")

5. **Elle veut mordre à belles dents.** She wants to go at it greedily. (literally, bite with beautiful teeth)

6. **Il est hardi comme un coq sur son fumier.** He's a show-off, brazen. (literally, as a rooster on his own dung)

7. **Elle était dans ses petits souliers.** She was uncomfortable, ill at ease. (literally, in her little shoes)

8. **Il ne faut pas déshabiller Pierre pour habiller Paul.** You shouldn't borrow more money in order to pay a debt. You shouldn't take money from Peter to pay Paul. (literally, undress Peter to dress Paul)

9. **J'ai un chat dans la gorge.** I have a frog in my throat. (literally, a cat in my throat)

10. **On a fait le pied de grue.** We hung around. (literally, stood on one foot like a crane)

Le je-m'en-foutisme et le jusqu'au-boutisme

For all of their wariness of new American words, the French allow themselves a lot of creativity in making up new French words and recombining old French words to make new ones. *Qu'en dira-t-on?* started as a question, "What will people say?" (literally, what will one say about it?). Then it became a noun: *le qu'en-dira-t-on*, "the gossip." It's always referred to disparagingly.

Je m'en fous is "I don't give a damn." Then that led to *le je-m'en-foutisme*, and the people with that attitude became *les je-m'en-foutistes*. Instead of saying *Je m'en fous*, you can say less forcefully *Je m'en fiche*, "I don't care." And in that case you can talk about *le je-m'en-fichisme* and *les je-m'en-fichistes*.

At the other extreme are the *jusqu'au-boutistes*. Literally, these people keep going until the end. They are the hardliners and sometimes extremists. *Le jusqu'au-boutisme* is often admired because *les jusqu'au-boutistes* follow through with their ideas.

English has borrowed many of the French multiple-word expressions, for example: *aide-mémoire, aide-de-camp, sang-froid, tour de force, avant-garde, pied-à-terre,* and *prêt-à porter.* The next step is for the words to meld into one new word such as *avoirdupois.* "*Avoirdupois*" suggests middle-aged spread and to have "*avoirdupois*" uses "to have" twice because *avoir* has been camouflaged in the new word.

TOP TEN Expressions with Multiple-Word Nouns

1. **Ils sont en tête-à-tête.** They're having a private conversation. (literally, head-to-head)

2. **C'est un touche-à-tout.** He/She dabbles in everything. (literally, touches everything)

3. **Il se soucie trop du qu'en-dira-t-on.** He's too worried about what others think. (literally, about the "what will one say")

4. **C'est du je-m'en-foutisme.** That's just blowing it off. (I-don't-give-a-fuckism)

5. **Il a une attitude de laisser-faire.** He has a laissez-faire attitude. As a policy, minimal government interference in economic policy. (literally, let do)

6. **Il est jusqu'au-boutiste.** He's a hardliner. (a right-through-to-the-ender)

7. **On va prendre un pousse-café.** We're going to have an after-dinner liqueur. (literally, a push-coffee; it follows coffee down the throat)

8. **C'est du déjà vu.** It's déjà vu. (literally, already seen)

9. **Il le fait à la va-comme-je-te-pousse.** He does it any old how. (literally, like the go-as-I-push-you)

10. **Ils le font toujours à la va-vite.** They always do it hastily. (literally, in the go-fast way)

Il recule pour mieux sauter

Reculer pour mieux sauter is a very effective image for taking your time and waiting for the right moment. Some of the most richly suggestive French metaphors deal with strategies and responses for dealing with difficult situations. *Il hurle avec les loups* is a reflection of peer pressure. Someone howls with the wolves instead of taking a stand and doing the right thing. With *Il hurle à la lune* he's doing better, howling at the moon, taking an independent stand, but in the sense that it doesn't do any good. *Il prend la lune avec les dents* means he's totally unrealistic, trying to take the moon in his teeth.

TOP TEN Expressions for Dealing with Something

1. **Il lui parle à brûle-pourpoint.** He asks him point-blank. (literally, close enough to burn his doublet)

2. **Il lui pose un lapin.** He stands him/her up. (Literally, he leaves him/her a rabbit.)

3. **Il prend la lune avec les dents.** He tries to do the impossible. (literally, takes the moon in his teeth; from Rabelais)

4. **Il recule pour mieux sauter.** He's waiting for the right moment. (Literally, he's backing up to take a better jump.)

5. **Il tire la couverture à lui.** He tries to get the best deal for himself. (literally, pulls the bedcover to his side)

6. **Il hurle avec les loups.** He joins in the unfair behavior along with the others by conformity. (literally, howls with the wolves)

7. **Ils font des gorges chaudes.** They're having a good laugh at someone's expense. (literally, warm throats)

8. **Il hurle à la lune.** He speaks truth to power but it's no use. (Literally, he howls at the moon.)

9. **C'est toujours donnant-donnant.** He always gives with the expectation of getting something in return, tit for tat. (literally, giving-giving)

10. **Il fait d'une pierre deux coups.** He kills two birds with one stone. (literally, one stone, two blows)

La vie en rose, vert et blanc

"La vie en rose" is a 1942 Edith Piaf song about romantic love and optimism, and *Ma vie en rose* is a 1997 movie by Alain Berliner about a seven-year-old boy who dresses as a girl.

Expressions with colors aren't necessarily the same in French and English. Fear can be green in French and white in English. And in the case of *un blanc-bec*, a white beak is "a greenhorn." In French you usually go red or blue with rage, *rouge de colère, bleu de colère*, rather than turning purple, but you can go purple with embarrassment, *On devient pourpre*.

In French it's possible to make a pun on an orange (yellow) traffic light and an orange. *Il est passé à l'orange bien mûre* means that someone went through a light that had just turned red, although if he got a ticket he might argue that the light was still yellow. He went through when the light was a very ripe orange.

TOP TEN Colorful States

1. **Ils voient la vie en rose.** They see life through rose-colored glasses. (pink)

2. **Il sourit jaune.** He's giving a sickly smile. (yellow)

3. **Elle était rouge de colère.** She was flushed with anger. (red)

4. **Il était vert de peur.** He was white with fear. (green)

5. **Il est noir.** He's dead drunk. (black)

6. **C'est un blanc-bec.** He's a greenhorn. (white)

7. **Il est devenu pourpre.** His face flushed with embarrassment. (purple)

8. **Il n'y voit que du bleu.** He doesn't get it. He doesn't notice a thing. (blue)

9. **Ils font grise mine.** They have long faces. (gray)

10. **Il est passé à l'orange bien mûre.** He went through a red light (ripe orange) but claimed it was still yellow.

Les Français, ils ont un certain je-ne-sais-quoi?

The French attitude to sex may seem blasé to Americans, but a Franco-American study of sexual habits showed that the stereotype of the French as having more infidelity and kinkier sex has no basis in reality. In spite of ideas about American puritanism and French *libertinage*, French and American sexual behavior patterns are actually very similar. (*L'Express*, 7–13 June, 2001 p. 54)

To Americans, the expression *une femme d'un certain âge* in the Quick Fixes section suggests a woman in her fifties or sixties trying with artifice to look as if she's in her twenties or thirties. It's a classic euphemism. But then just saying something in French makes it sound more suggestive to an American ear. *Un rendez-vous* sounds more romantic than a meeting, but in French *un rendez-vous* can just mean an "appointment." *Sur rendez-vous* means "by appointment" and applies to all kinds of business and medical appointments. Words like *scandale* and *affaire* are often spelled the French way in English to make them look naughtier. English has borrowed expressions such as *une affaire du cœur*, "a love affair"; *une femme fatale*, "a seductive woman"; *le droit du seigneur*, the right of a feudal lord to have sexual relations with a vassal's wife on their wedding night; and *entre nous*, "just between us." *Vive la différence* seems to be overdone as a French quotation in English, and it tends to be used in English as a justification of sexual stereotypes. While *au naturel* usually just refers in French to food that's cooked in a simple way, it's invariably used by English speakers to mean "in the nude."

TOP TEN French Expressions That Sound Particularly French to Americans

1. **Elle a un certain je-ne-sais-quoi.** She has a certain something. (Literally, I don't know what.)

2. **Vive la différence.** Long live the difference.

3. **Elle lui envoie des billets-doux.** She sends him love letters.

4. **Ils ont une amitié amoureuse.** They have a loving friendship.

5. **C'est une passade.** It's a fling. (a passing love affair)

6. **C'était le coup de foudre.** It was love at first sight. (literally, the thunderclap)

7. **C'est un chaud lapin.** He's oversexed. (literally, a hot rabbit)

8. **Cherchez la femme.** There's a woman at the bottom of it. Find her and solve the mystery. (Literally, look for the woman.)

9. **Ils se font les yeux doux.** They're making eyes at each other. (literally, making soft or sweet eyes)

10. **Ils étaient au naturel.** They were served without dressing. (They were naked.)

L'amour fou

Attitudes may be different even if practices aren't. The French go in more for romance, tenderness, and nuance in the way they talk. And *l'amour fou*, "wild passion," is another French term used in English. When pulling the petals off a daisy, Americans just say "He loves me. He loves me not" or "She loves me. She loves me not." The French go through a cycle of five petals that includes *à la folie*. Audrey Tautou starred in the 2002 French movie, *A la folie, pas du tout* that was given the English title, "He loves me. He loves me not."

The French Way with a Daisy

1. **Il/Elle m'aime.** He/She loves me.

2. **Un peu.** A little.

3. **Beaucoup.** A lot.

4. **A la folie.** Like crazy.

5. **Pas du tout.** Not at all.

🎼 Rehearsal Time

Choose the answer that best corresponds to the expression.

1. Si nous faisons le pont, nous
   a. courbons le dos
   b. avons quatre jours de vacances
   c. allons nous ennuyer

2. Si vous prenez un bain de jouvence,
   a. vous serez très propre
   b. vous allez vieillir
   c. vous allez rajeunir

3. Quand vous avez l'esprit de corps
   a. vous vous entendez bien avec les autres membres de l'équipe
   b. vous êtes bien dans votre corps
   c. vous aimez les mots d'esprit

4. Une éminence grise, c'est
   a. quelqu'un qui donne des conseils au président
   b. un rocher
   c. un très vieux magistrat

5. Il y a anguille sous roche.
   a. Il est possible de coudre en toutes circonstances.
   b. Il y a une chose dissimulée qu'on soupçonne.
   c. Les plus petits poissons savent se cacher.

6. Le dindon de la farce c'est
   a. le repas traditionnel du premier décembre
   b. la victime
   c. un personnage comique

7. Il faut ménager la chèvre et le chou.
   a. La viande se mange avec les légumes.
   b. Il est bon de vivre à la ferme.
   c. Il faut concilier les intérêts contradictoires.

8. Elle a du chien.
   a. Elle est attirante.
   b. Elle n'est pas belle.
   c. Elle veut se venger.

9. C'est une pierre dans mon jardin parce que
   a. vous m'avez insulté
   b. vous m'avez expliqué comment faire pousser les fleurs
   c. nous allons pouvoir travailler ensemble

10. Elle a dit "Un ange passe," quand
    a. vous lui avez effleuré le bras si tendrement
    b. il y avait une pause dans la conversation
    c. il fallait partir

Complete the sentences with the expressions below.

le trou normand	le pied de grue
à la lune	je-m'en-foutiste
dans le pétrin	le coup de foudre
dans ses petits souliers	pour mieux sauter
des gorges chaudes	un poil dans la main

11. Quand ils boivent du calvados entre les plats, c'est _____.

12. Vous êtes _____ maintenant. Tout va mal. Je ne sais pas comment vous allez en sortir.

13. Nous n'avons rien à faire ici et nous nous ennuyons à mourir. On ne va pas rester à faire _____.

14. Qu'est-ce qu'il est paresseux! Il a _____.

15. Elle semble y avoir renoncé, mais n'y croyez pas. En réalité elle recule _____.

16. Je ne sais pas pourquoi ils se moquent de moi, mais de toute façon ils font _____.

17. La première fois qu'elle l'a vu, elle était amoureuse de lui. C'était _____.

18. Il semblait être très mal à l'aise. Il était _____ parce qu'il ne savait pas comment il fallait se comporter.

19. Elle tient bon et continue à faire des revendications mais tout le monde croit qu'elle hurle _____.

20. Peut-être qu'ils s'en soucient, mais à mon avis ils ont une attitude tout à fait _____.

Wit

Play with Language
the French Way

Preview

1. If you hear *Il a tout pour plaire*, what are the two different ways that this can be interpreted?

2. What's the line that French panhandlers use when they hit you up for money?

3. What do French customs officials most often say when asking if you have anything to declare?

4. What is meant by *Il ne faut pas prendre les enfants du Bon Dieu pour des canards sauvages*?

5. In *Le Cid* how does Chimène tell Rodrigue that she loves him without using the word "love"?

6. Using the negative, how do you say something is difficult?

7. Using the negative, how do you say something is easy?

8. If something is *pas terrible*, is it bad or good?

9. What is meant by *Ce n'est pas de la petite bière*?

10. While maintaining the meaning of the French expression *Il n'a pas inventé la poudre*, what other things could you substitute for *la poudre*?

11. What does it mean if someone says *Je ne crache pas dessus*?

12. How do you say "I wasn't born yesterday" in French?

13. How well do people know each other when you hear that *Ils n'ont pas gardé les cochons ensemble*?

14. Give an example of an ironic use of language by Voltaire.

15. What is meant by *C'est le bouquet*?

16. Where would you be if someone said to you, *Je vais vous apporter des oranges*?

17. Why does *Je fais comme Charles* mean "I'm waiting"?

18. Who is *Marianne*, and where can you find a statue of her?

19. Who is *Jules* in the expression *C'est son jules*?

20. What name rhymes with *A la tienne* in the toast?

Expressing your sense of humor in another language is an important milestone. You don't need a repertoire of French jokes, but you do need playfulness, understatement, exaggeration, and always lots of irony. The French express irony by saying what something isn't instead of what it is. In English we also express irony by using the negative, but the French just do it a whole lot more often.

In French, if you want to say someone is arrogant, say he doesn't think he's a nobody. If you want to say he's smart, say he's not stupid. If things are going badly, say they are not going well. If you want to say yes, say that you do not say no.

An example of the French kind of irony is the expression, *Il ne faut pas prendre les enfants du Bon Dieu pour des canards sauvages.* "You shouldn't mistake God's children for wild ducks," which is a fancy way of saying, "Don't go looking for trouble."

By and large, using negatives to express positives implies a rueful take on human nature. Marcel Pagnol was a master of understatement, as well as of exaggeration, a trait people from Marseille are famous for. In his play *Marius*, Pagnol has one character insult another, saying, «*Quand on fera danser les couillons, tu ne seras pas dans l'orchestre.*» "When they get the idiots to dance, you won't be sitting in the orchestra" —an exaggerated understatement as a way of telling someone he's an idiot.

The French use the negative even when they are not trying to be ironic. For example, the French customs official will ask you *Vous n'avez rien à déclarer?* "You don't have anything to declare?" The American customs official says "Do you have anything to declare?" In comparing the way children are prompted to say thank you, we saw that French parents say *On ne dit pas merci?* while American parents say "What do you say?" And the cashier's line *Vous n'avez pas la monnaie?* in a French store would be "Do you have change?" in an American store. French panhandlers used to beg *Vous n'auriez pas deux francs?* but now they ask for more, *Vous n'auriez pas un euro?*—still using the negative. American panhandlers are more likely to say "Do you have any spare change?" *Vous n'aurez pas la conscience tranquille* is the French way of saying you'll have a guilty conscience.

Understatement was already alive and well in seventeenth-century France when Corneille wrote *Le Cid*. Rodrigue gets a clue that Chimène loves him madly when she says very seriously, «*Va. Je ne te hais point,*» literally, "Go. I don't hate you at all." Chimène was not trying to be funny, but it's just a short step from Chimène's understatement to the offhand wit of current expressions such as *Je ne le porte pas dans mon cœur*, meaning "I loathe him," literally, "I don't hold him in my heart."

The tour leader of a group of skiers was so arrogant that another skier said about him, «*Il ne se prend pas pour de la merde,*» literally, "He doesn't mistake himself for shit," meaning that he thinks he's hot shit. The intimidating *chef* suddenly seemed laughable.

Ce n'est pas la mer à boire

Some understated reactions are just two words long. If something is very good, you say *Pas mal!* "Well done!" If something is annoying, you can say *Pas marrant!* "Not funny!" If it's inconvenient, you can say *Pas commode*.

If you want to say something is hard, say *Pas facile* or *Ce n'est pas facile*. You can then work up to something more complicated. If something is easy, say *Ce n'est pas la mer à boire*. If something is a big deal, you can understate to exaggerate: *Ce n'est pas de la petite bière*.

TOP TEN   Ways to Say What It Isn't

1. **Ce n'est pas fameux.** It's terrible. (not great)

2. **Ce n'est pas sorcier.** It's a cinch. (not mysteriously difficult)

3. **Ce n'est pas facile.** It's hard. (not easy)

4. **Ce n'est pas évident.** It's difficult. It looks hard to do. (not obvious)

5. **Ce n'est pas exclu.** It's possible. (not out of the question)

6. **Ce n'est pas donné.** It's expensive. (not free)

7. **Ce n'est pas terrible.** It's bad. (not terrific; here, *terrible* means "terrific")

8. **Ce n'est pas tous les jours fête.** It's pretty boring around here. (not a holiday every day)

9. **Ce n'est pas de la petite bière.** It's a big deal. (not small beer)

10. **Ce n'est pas la mer à boire.** It's fairly straightforward. (not like drinking the ocean)

TOP TEN Ways to Say What Someone Isn't

1. **Il n'est pas brillant.** He's stupid. (not brilliant)

2. **Elle n'est pas bête.** She's brilliant. (not stupid)

3. **Il n'est pas méchant.** He's harmless. (not mean)

4. **Elle n'est pas sérieuse.** She's fickle and unreliable. (not serious)

5. **Il n'est pas mal de sa personne.** He's good-looking. (not bad-looking)

6. **Elle n'a pas inventé la poudre.** She's dumb. (She didn't invent gunpowder.) **Il n'a pas inventé le fil à couper le beurre.** He's stupid. (He didn't invent the wire for cutting butter.) The things he or she didn't invent can vary: *la poudre, l'eau chaude, le vin chaud, les œufs durs.*

7. **Il ne se foule pas la rate.** He takes it easy. (doesn't strain his spleen)

8. **Elle ne manque pas de culot.** She's got a nerve. (doesn't lack cheekiness)

9. **Il n'a pas l'air d'un enfant de chœur.** He looks like he knows his way around. (doesn't look like a choirboy)

10. **Elle n'a pas les deux pieds dans le même sabot.** She's a live wire. (doesn't have both feet in the same wooden shoe)

TOP TEN Ways to Say What's Not Happening

1. **Ça ne se bouscule pas.** There's hardly anyone here. (People aren't bumping into each other.)

2. **Ça ne tourne pas rond.** There's something wrong here. I smell something fishy. (It's not turning in a circle.)

3. **On ne court pas après.** We could let it go. We're not interested. (not running after it)

4. **Vous n'y allez pas par quatre chemins.** You're getting right to the point. (You're not taking four different roads.)

5. **Il n'y a pas le feu.** Take your time. (There isn't a fire.)

6. **Il ne faut pas couper les cheveux en quatre.** Let's focus on the big picture. It's not worth splitting hairs. (cutting hairs in four)

7. **Il n'y a pas de quoi faire des histoires.** It's simple enough. No big deal. (nothing to make a fuss about)

8. **On n'arrête pas le progrès.** So that's progress? This is a step backward. (You can't stop progress.)

9. **Ne vous gênez pas.** I see that you are making yourself right at home. (Ironic advice: don't hang back.)

10. **Je ne vous retiens pas.** Time for you to leave. Here's your hat. (I'm not detaining you.)

TOP TEN Ironic Assessments

1. **Je ne suis pas de la dernière pluie.** I know what's really going on. I wasn't born yesterday. (wasn't born with the last rain)

2. **On ne peut rien vous cacher.** You finally noticed. (I can't hide anything from you.)

3. **Une hirondelle ne fait pas le printemps.** Things look a little better, but you can't tell yet. (One swallow doesn't make it springtime.)

4. **On ne vit pas de l'air du temps.** You need money to live. (You can't live on thin air.)

5. **Ce n'est pas un cadeau.** It's annoying. (not a gift)

6. **Ce n'est pas du gâteau.** It's hard to do. (not a piece of cake)

7. **Ce n'est pas un pur esprit.** He/She has physical needs as well. (not just a pure spirit)

8. **Ils n'ont pas gardé les cochons ensemble.** They know each other slightly. (didn't take care of the pigs together)

9. **Il n'est pas en odeur de sainteté auprès de lui.** He's in the doghouse. He's out of favor with him. (He doesn't smell saintly to him.)

10. **Je ne crache pas dessus.** I think well of it. (I'm not spitting on it.)

Ça promet

You can also say something positively to mean the opposite. In the case of expressions such as *Il a tout pour plaire* (or *Elle a tout pour plaire*) you can't be sure, out of context, whether to take the expression at face value or ironically. It might mean, "He's got everything going for him." But recently, it has come to mean the opposite. Ironically, it refers to a loser.

If you really want to make a point, follow Voltaire. Say the opposite of what you mean. When Voltaire's Candide is taken to a dungeon, it is described as an extremely cool place where *On n'était jamais incommodé du soleil*, "One was never bothered by the sun." Things always turned out for the worst in *le meilleur des mondes possibles*, "the best of all possible worlds."

You can make your point strongly by saying the opposite of what you mean. If something is the most far-fetched thing you've ever heard of, you can say *C'est la meilleure...*, literally, "It's the best . . .". It really means "That's a good one!" If someone will talk your head off, say *Il a la langue bien pendue*, literally, "His tongue is well hung, well attached."

If someone gives you only a tiny scrap of paper to write on, you can say *Merci, vous êtes bien bon*, "Thank you, you're very kind." If you expect that things are going to get worse, say *Ça promet*, "Things look promising," meaning "Uh-oh."

TOP TEN Examples of Basic Irony

1. **C'est du joli.** What a mess. (pretty)

2. **Tu es joli(e).** You look a mess. (pretty)

3. **C'est le bouquet.** That's the last straw. (the bouquet)

4. **C'est la meilleure!** That's the worst idea I've heard! (the best)

5. **Ça promet.** It's going to get worse. (It's promising.)

6. **Mes compliments.** Now look what you've done. (Congratulations.)

7. **La belle affaire.** That's a fine state of affairs. (a beautiful situation)

8. **C'est bien fait pour lui.** He had it coming. (well done for him)

9. **Merci, tu es bien bon(ne).** Is that the best you could do? (Thanks, you're very kind.)

10. **Il est dans un bel état.** He's in a mess. (a fine state)

L'espoir fait vivre

If you want to say that it's naive to be hopeful, you can say *L'espoir fait vivre*, "Hope keeps one alive." *Je veux bien le croire* expresses skepticism, although it sounds as though you want to believe what you're told. It's more along the lines of "I'll believe it when I see it."

On s'appelle et on se fait une bouffe and *Je vais vous apporter des oranges* are expressions that make fun of conventional platitudes. Usually the expression *On s'appelle et on se fait une bouffe* (Let's get together some time) makes fun of vague promises people make each other of getting together for a meal. But you can say it with the ironic meaning to a friend you really would like to have dinner with. If you want to say that you are going to visit someone in the hospital or in prison you can say *Je vais lui apporter des oranges.* *Ne compte pas sur moi pour t'apporter des oranges* means "Don't expect me to help you." The expression *Je vais vous apporter des oranges* originated at the end of the nineteenth century when bringing oranges was considered the appropriate way to comfort someone who was sick or in the hospital. Because of both the expression and the tradition, friends still bring oranges in such circumstances.

TOP TEN Examples of Ironic Detachment

1. **En voilà une idée.** That's a weird idea. (Now there's an idea.)

2. **Je veux bien le croire.** I'm not so sure. (I'd like to think so.)

3. **L'espoir fait vivre.** You can always hope. (Hope keeps one alive.)

4. **Vous serez bien avancé(e).** A lot of good that will do. (You'd really be getting ahead.)

5. **Où il y a de la gêne, il n'y a pas de plaisir.** Some people act pretty entitled. (If you feel ill at ease, you can't enjoy yourself.)

6. **C'est tout nouveau, tout beau.** The novelty will soon wear off. (It's all new and beautiful.)

7. **La mariée est trop belle.** It's too good to be true. (The bride is too beautiful.)

8. **On s'appelle et on se fait une bouffe.** Let's stay in touch. (Let's call each other and get together for a bite to eat.)

9. **Je vais vous apporter des oranges.** I'll visit you in prison. I'll visit you in the hospital. (I'm going to bring you some oranges.)

10. **Il a avalé son acte de naissance.** He died, kicked the bucket. (He swallowed his birth certificate.)

Je fais comme Charles

The French love a far-fetched pun. *Je fais comme Charles* means *J'attends*, "I'm waiting." It would be impossible for the uninitiated to understand the hidden progression in the pun *Je fais comme*

Charles: *Charlatan, Charles attend, J'attends comme Charles*, ending up with *Je fais comme Charles*.

The names *Marianne* and *Jules* have particular significance in French. Marianne is a nickname for the Republic, and there is a statue of her in every town hall. She is a combination of a glorified symbol of France since 1848 and a pop icon. France currently has a different model for Marianne each year. Brigitte Bardot was the first of many well-known Frenchwomen, including Catherine Deneuve and Mireille Matthieu, who have served as models for Marianne. In recent years the Mariannes have included Laetitia Casta, a movie star and Victoria's Secret model, whose choice proved particularly controversial when it was discovered that she had moved to London; an anonymous young woman of North African descent chosen as an emblem of France as a multiethnic society; and a television personality, Evelyne Thomas. *Jules* is a generic name for "boyfriend." *C'est son jules* means "That's her boyfriend."

The French also like to make rhymes. Often the rhyming word is a man's name, as in *Tout juste, Auguste* and *Relaxe, Max*. *A la tienne, Etienne* is a well-known toast. The expressions don't always have to rhyme with names, however. There's also *Tu l'as dit, bouffi*. "You said it, puffy." *Je veux, mon neveu*. "I'd like to, my nephew." *T'en fais pas, Papa*. "Don't worry."

When I was wondering if French had a rhyme like "Geeze, Louise" that included a woman's name, I thought of Jacques Prévert's line, *Rappelle-toi, Barbara*. "Remember, Barbara." Prévert apparently liked word play so much that *Barbara*, a serious poem about the bombing of the port of Brest, starts with the rhyme *Rappelle-toi, Barbara*. Another rhyming expression with a woman's name is *Ça glisse, Alice*.

In Jean-Luc Godard's movie *Pierrot le fou*, Jean-Paul Belmondo revs up his car and says alliteratively «*Allons-y, Alonzo*» and the subtitle is *Let's Go, Daddy-O*. You won't find anyone named Alonzo in the film, of course. You can try out these expressions anytime.

TOP TEN Expressions That Rhyme with Names

1. **Ça glisse, Alice.** Watch out. It's slippery.

2. **Tu as tort, Totor.** You're wrong.

3. **Tout juste, Auguste.** Just made it. That was close.

4. **A la tienne, Etienne.** Cheers.

5. **Fonce, Alphonse.** Full steam ahead. Let's get a move on. (The subtitle in Godard's *A bout de souffle* is *Straight Ahead, Fred.*)

6. **Tu parles, Charles.** You bet.

7. **A l'aise, Blaise.** Nothing to worry about.

8. **Cool, Raoul.** Calm down. Cool it.

9. **Relaxe, Max.** Take it easy.

10. **Recule, Hercule.** Step back. Out of my way.

Rehearsal Time

To sound more ironic, say the same thing using an idiom that's in the negative. For example, *C'est formidable.* Ce n'est pas fameux.

1. C'est bon.

2. On s'ennuie ici.

3. Elle est audacieuse.

4. C'est difficile.

5. C'est compliqué.

6. C'est possible.

7. C'est cher.

8. C'est très important.

9. Elle est brillante.

10. Il est bête.

Choose the expression that's closest in meaning.

11. Il y a peu de monde ici aujourd'hui.
    a. Ça ne se bouscule pas.
    b. Ça ne tourne pas rond.
    c. Ça ne se voit pas.

12. Il faut regarder la situation dans son ensemble.
    a. On ne court pas après.
    b. Vous n'y allez pas par quatre chemins.
    c. Il ne faut pas couper les cheveux en quatre.

13. C'est assez simple.
    a. Ce n'est pas facile.
    b. Ce n'est pas un cadeau.
    c. Il n'y a pas de quoi faire des histoires.

14. Tu peux prendre ton temps.
    a. Il n'y a pas le feu.
    b. Tu n'as pas les deux pieds dans le même sabot.
    c. Tu es dans un bel état.

15. Je suis assez enthousiaste.
    a. On n'arrête pas le progrès.
    b. Ne vous gênez pas.
    c. Je ne crache pas dessus.

Complete the expression with the appropriate name.

16. A la tienne _____

17. Ça glisse _____

18. Allons-y _____

19. Tout juste _____

20. On fonce _____

Improvisation

Build on Famous French Quotations to Create Your Own Expressions

1. What is the motto of France?

2. What is meant by *Il est interdit d'interdire*, and where did this slogan come from?

3. What does *Touche pas à mon pote* mean, and of what organization is it the slogan?

4. What is meant by *A la guerre comme à la guerre*?

5. Can you explain *Si jeunesse savait, si vieillesse pouvait?*

6. Cite a French superstition that's different from an American one.

7. What is *un violon d'Ingres?*

8. What did Henry IV mean by *Paris vaut bien une messe?*

9. Who is supposed to have said *S'ils n'ont pas de pain, qu'ils mangent de la brioche?*

10. Who said *Du sublime au ridicule, il n'y a qu'un pas?*

11. Who said *La France ne peut être la France sans la grandeur?*

12. What French poet said *Cueillez dès aujourd'hui les roses de la vie?*

13. Whose book ended with the words *Il faut cultiver notre jardin?*

14. Who wrote a letter that started with the words *J'accuse?*

15. What philosopher is famous for saying *Je pense donc je suis?*

16. What famous French writer responded three centuries later with *Je me révolte, donc nous sommes?*

17. What French writer started the field of gender studies by writing *On n'est pas née femme, on le devient?*

18. What philosophy is based on the theory *L'existence précède l'essence?*

19. What is meant by *Qui vit sans folie n'est pas si sage qu'il croit?*

20. Explain *Un dessert sans fromage est une belle à qui il manque un œil.*

French writers, comics, and advertising executives rely constantly on a repertoire of quotations and sayings that they assume most French-speaking adults know. The cadence of these expressions is often the cadence of spoken French. French quotations both reflect and influence the way French is spoken.

Sometimes the words of modern French voices sound like seventeenth-century *maximes*. To give a few examples: *Il y a de la malchance à n'être pas aimé. Il y a du malheur à ne point aimer.* "It's unlucky not to be loved. It's a calamity not to love at all" (Albert Camus). *Se vouloir libre, c'est aussi vouloir les autres libres.* "To want to be free is to want others to be free" (Simone de Beauvoir). *Quand les riches font la guerre, ce sont les pauvres qui meurent.* "When the rich make war, it's the poor who die" (Jean-Paul Sartre). Because prose writers and poets try to capture the rhythms of everyday spoken language, what they write also influences the spoken language. Poems, songs, and advertising slogans are committed to memory, and the cycle continues.

In this chapter, I present French examples of *forme et fond*, "style and substance," that will serve as models that will help you express yourself in your own words. As always, the point is not to try to learn all of the top ten lists by heart, but to acquire some French expressions that interest you while you get a feeling for French from the others. Enjoy and improvise.

TOP TEN Slogans and Mottoes

In the list below, the first five slogans came into the French language during the student protests in Paris in May 1968.

1. **Faites l'amour, pas la guerre.** Make love, not war.

2. **Il est interdit d'interdire.** Forbidding forbidden.

3. **L'imagination prend le pouvoir.** The imagination seizes power.

4. **Prenons nos désirs pour la réalité.** Let's take our wishes for reality.

5. **Sous les pavés, la plage.** Under the cobblestones, the beach.

6. **Touche pas à mon pote.** Leave my pal alone. (slogan of S.O.S. Racisme, an antiracist group)

7. **Liberté, Egalité, Fraternité.** Liberty, Equality, Fraternity. (motto of France)

8. **Je flotte et ne sombre pas.** (*Fluctuat nec mergitur.*) I float and I don't sink. (motto of Paris)

9. **Simplicité est ma devise.** Simplicity is my motto.

10. **Plutôt souffrir que mourir, c'est la devise des hommes.** Better to suffer than to die, that's the motto of mankind. (La Fontaine)

TOP TEN Proverbs and Sayings

1. **A la guerre comme à la guerre.** You have to take things as they come.

2. **Un(e) de perdu(e), dix de retrouvé(e)s.** There's a lot of fish in the sea.

3. **Ce que femme veut, Dieu le veut.** What a woman wants, God wants.

4. **C'est en forgeant qu'on devient forgeron.** Practice makes perfect.

5. **Des goûts et des couleurs, il ne faut pas discuter.** You can't argue with taste.

6. **L'habit ne fait pas le moine.** Clothes don't make the man. (Literally, the cowl doesn't make the monk.)

7. **On ne fait pas d'omelette sans casser des œufs.** You can't make an omelet without breaking eggs.

8. **Qui ne dit mot, consent.** If you don't object, you consent.

9. **Si jeunesse savait, si vieillesse pouvait.** If youth but knew, if old age but could.

10. **Tout comprendre, c'est tout pardonner.** To understand is to forgive.

TOP TEN Superstitions

Ce qui porte bonheur (good luck):

1. **Le trèfle à quatre feuilles porte bonheur.** A four-leaf clover is good luck.

2. **Marcher dans une crotte du pied gauche porte bonheur.** Walking in dung with the left foot is good luck.

3. **Un fer à cheval porte bonheur.** A horseshoe is good luck.

4. **Casser du verre blanc porte bonheur.** Breaking plain glass is good luck.

5. **Voir une coccinelle s'envoler annonce le beau temps.** Seeing a ladybird fly off means good weather ahead.

Ce qui porte malheur (bad luck):

6. **Etre treize personnes à table porte malheur.** Thirteen people at a meal is bad luck.

7. **Mettre le pain à l'envers porte malheur.** Putting bread upside down is bad luck.

8. **Ouvrir un parapluie à l'intérieur de la maison porte malheur.** Opening an umbrella inside a house is bad luck.

9. **Casser un miroir porte malheur.** Breaking a mirror is bad luck.

10. **Passer sous une échelle porte malheur.** Walking under a ladder is bad luck.

TOP TEN Puns, Real and Surreal

1. **Vous savez avec quoi on joue à pile ou face? Avec une pince et une gomme! Parce que la pince épile et la gomme efface.** (French comedian and actor Michel "Coluche" Colucci) Do you know what you play heads and tails (tail and head) with? With a pair of tweezers and an eraser. Because the tweezers tweeze (*épile/est pile* "is tails") and the eraser erases (*efface/est face* "is heads").

2. **Géricault: célèbre peintre français dont la trompette était le violon d'Ingres.** (Pierre Dac) Géricault: French painter whose trumpet was Ingres's violin. *Un violon d'Ingres,* "hobby," comes from the sideline of the painter Jean-Auguste-Dominique Ingres (1780–1867), who played the violin. *La trompette* is "trumpet," but the painter Théodore Géricault (1791–1824) did a famous painting of a horseman in the cavalry called *Le trompette* (*The Bugler*).

3. **Ne rien faire. Ça peut se dire, mais ça ne peut pas se faire.** (Raymond Devos) Not to do anything. You can say it, but you can't do it.

4. **Quand les verts voient rouge, ils votent blanc.** (Raymond Devos) When members of the Green Party get angry they don't vote. (*les verts,* "the green party"; *voir rouge,* "to see red"; *voter blanc,* "to leave the vote blank")

5. **Est-ce l'œuf, le père de la poule ou la poule, la mère de l'œuf?** (Raymond Devos) Is the egg the father of the hen, or is the hen the mother of the egg?

6. **Je suis adroit de la main gauche et je suis gauche de la main droite.** (Raymond Devos) I'm adroit with my left hand and gauche with my right hand.

7. **L'argent ne fait pas le bonheur de celui qui n'en a pas.** (Boris Vian) Money doesn't make you happy if you don't have any.

8. **Qui avale son parapluie marche forcément droit.** (Dada) He who swallows his umbrella has to walk straight.

9. **Partir, c'est mourir un peu, mais mourir, c'est partir beaucoup.** (Alphonse Allais) Leaving is dying a little, but dying is leaving a lot.

10. **Plus un citron est pressé, plus il se dépêche.** (Pierre Dac) The more a lemon is in a rush, the more he hurries. (*citron pressé*, "lemonade"; *une pêche*, "a peach")

TOP TEN Morals from Jean de la Fontaine's *Fables*

1. **Rien ne sert de courir, il faut partir à point.** It's no use running to catch up. You need to start on time. (*Le Lièvre et la Tortue*)

2. **Ils sont trop verts.** The grapes are too green to eat. A way of rationalizing so that you don't want what you can't have anyway. (*Le Renard et les Raisins*)

3. **C'est la mouche du coche.** Allusion to a person (the fly on the stagecoach) who manages to seem very busy and important while accomplishing nothing. (*Le Coche et la Mouche*)

4. **La raison du plus fort est toujours la meilleure.** The strongest person gets his own way. (*Le Loup et l'Agneau*)

5. **En toute chose il faut considérer la fin.** As you sow, so shall you reap. In everything you have to consider the purpose. (*Le Renard et le Bouc*)

6. **Aide-toi, le Ciel t'aidera.** The Lord helps those who help themselves. (*Le Chartier embourbé*)

7. **A l'œuvre, on connaît l'artisan.** You can tell the artisan from his work. (*Les Frelons et les Mouches à miel.*)

8. **Aucun chemin de fleurs ne conduit à la gloire.** There's no easy road to success. No path strewn with flowers leads to glory. (*Les Deux Aventuriers et le Talisman*)

9. **Plus fait douceur que violence.** Kindness is more effective than violence. (*Phébus et Borée*)

10. **Petit poisson deviendra grand.** Wait to see what he/she becomes. A little fish will become a big fish. (*Le Petit Poisson et le Pêcheur*)

TOP TEN Famous Historic Sayings

1. **Qui m'aime me suive.** May whoever loves me follow me. (Philippe VI in 1328. This became a slogan for a brand of jeans.)

2. **Paris vaut bien une messe.** Paris is worth saying a mass for. (attributed to Henry IV when he converted to Catholicism in order to become king)

3. **L'Etat c'est moi.** I am the state. (attributed to Louis XIV)

4. **S'ils n'ont pas de pain, qu'ils mangent de la brioche.** Let them eat cake. (attributed to Marie-Antoinette)

5. **Après moi, le déluge.** After me, it's all over. Who cares what happens then? (Literally, "After me, the flood"; usually attributed to Louis XV.)

6. **J'y suis. J'y reste.** I'm here. And I'm staying. (Marshal MacMahon at the siege of Sebastopol in 1855)

7. **Du sublime au ridicule, il n'y a qu'un pas.** From the sublime to the ridiculous is just one step. (Napoléon, *Le Mémorial de Sainte Hélène*)

8. **La France a perdu une bataille, elle n'a pas perdu la guerre.** France has lost a battle, but it has not lost the war. (Charles de Gaulle, London, July 1940)

9. **La France ne peut être la France sans la grandeur.** France cannot be France without its greatness. (Charles de Gaulle, *Mémoires de guerre*)

10. **La liberté de la presse présente des inconvénients. Mais moins que l'absence de liberté.** Freedom of the press has disadvantages. But fewer than its absence. (François Mitterand)

TOP TEN Quotations from French Writers

1. **Le scandale est souvent pire que le péché.** The scandal is often worse than the sin. (Marguerite de Navarre, *L'Heptaméron*)

2. **Cueillez dès aujourd'hui les roses de la vie.** Gather ye rosebuds while ye may. (Pierre de Ronsard, *Sonnets pour Hélène*. Ronsard is quoted by the Robin Williams character in the movie *Dead Poets Society*, which became a cult hit in France.)

3. **Tarte à la crème.** Saying *tarte à la crème*, "cream pie," means "They are saying the same old thing." (Molière, *L'Ecole des*

femmes. Tarte à la crème was repeated in *La Critique de l'Ecole des femmes* to indicate any clichéd formula.)

4. **Il faut cultiver notre jardin.** We must cultivate our garden. (Last words of the book in Voltaire's *Candide*. Voltaire thought progress was possible through action rather than metaphysical speculation.)

5. **Ecrasons l'infâme.** Stamp out infamy. Don't let the bastards get you. (Voltaire often ended his letters with *Ecrasons l'infâme*, referring to his enemies, the fanatics.)

6. **Bon appétit, messieurs!** Enjoy your meal, Gentlemen. (Victor Hugo, *Ruy Blas*. An allusion to corruption, it's an aside used ironically to point out hypocrisy.)

7. **J'accuse.** I accuse. (Emile Zola. Title and also the first words of an open letter in the newspaper *L'Aurore*, January 13, 1898, about the Dreyfus affair. Zola accuses the government of sacrificing Alfred Dreyfus's rights as a citizen for *la raison d'Etat.*)

8. **Laissons les jolies femmes aux hommes sans imagination.** Beautiful women should be reserved for men who don't have any imagination. (Literally, let's leave beautiful women to men without imagination.) (Marcel Proust, *La Fugitive* or *Albertine disparue*)

9. **Si vous n'êtes pas capable d'un peu de sorcellerie, ce n'est pas la peine de vous mêler de cuisine.** If you aren't up to a bit of magic, it's not worth getting involved in cooking. (Colette, *Prisons et paradis*)

10. **Tout bonheur est une innocence.** All happiness is a form of innocence. (Marguerite Yourcenar, *Alexis ou le traité du vain combat*)

TOP TEN   Philosophical Touchstones

1. **Que sais-je?** What do I know? (Michel de Montaigne, *Les Essais*, Livre II. An example of Montaigne's skepticism, his belief in the fallibility of reason. Montaigne wrote personal essays because he saw truth as subjective.)

2. **Je pense donc je suis.** I think therefore I am. (René Descartes, *Discours de la méthode*)

3. **Le cœur a ses raisons que la raison ne connaît point.** The heart has its reasons that reason doesn't know. (Blaise Pascal, *Pensées*)

4. **La nature a fait l'homme heureux et bon, mais... la société le déprave et le rend misérable.** Nature made man happy and good, but . . . life in society made him depraved and miserable. (Rousseau, *Rousseau juge de Jean-Jacques*)

5. **Comment peut-on être persan?** How can one be Persian? (Montesquieu, from *Lettres persanes*, a satire of the frivolity of Parisians)

6. **Il n'y a qu'un devoir, c'est d'être heureux.** There's only one duty, to be happy. (Diderot, *Entretiens*)

7. **Je me révolte donc nous sommes.** I rebel, therefore we are. (Albert Camus, *L'Homme révolté*, an affirmation of free will and a reference to Descartes)

8. **On n'est pas née femme, on le devient.** One is not born a woman, one becomes one. (Simone de Beauvoir in *Le Deuxième Sexe*, her work that was considered the birth of gender studies.)

9. **L'existence précède l'essence.** Existence precedes essence. (Jean-Paul Sartre, *L'existentialisme est un humanisme*, a tenet of existentialism. Sartre believed that there was no preexisting human nature.)

10. **Chaque objet est le miroir de tous les autres.** Each object is a mirror of all others. (Merleau-Ponty, *Phénoménologie de la perception*)

TOP TEN Maxims

From La Rochefoucauld, *Maximes*:

1. **Qui vit sans folie n'est pas si sage qu'il croit.** He who lives without folly is not as wise as he thinks.

2. **L'hypocrisie est un hommage que le vice rend à la vertu.** Hypocrisy is the homage that vice renders to virtue.

3. **On aime mieux dire du mal de soi-même que de n'en point parler.** One would rather speak ill of oneself than not talk about oneself at all.

4. **Tout le monde se plaint de sa mémoire mais personne ne se plaint de son jugement.** Everyone complains about his memory, but no one complains about his judgment.

5. **Il est plus aisé d'être sage pour les autres que de l'être pour soi-même.** It's easier to tell others what to do than to know what to do oneself. (Literally, it's easier to be wise for others than for oneself.)

From Brillat-Savarin, *Physiologie du goût*:

6. **La destinée des nations dépend de la façon dont elles se nourrissent.** The destiny of nations depends on how they eat.

7. **Dis-moi ce que tu manges, je te dirai ce que tu es.** You are what you eat.

8. **La découverte d'un mets nouveau fait plus pour le bonheur du genre humain que la découverte d'une étoile.** The discovery of a new food does more for the happiness of the human race than the discovery of a star.

9. **Ceux qui s'indigèrent ou qui s'enivrent ne savent ni boire ni manger.** Those who get indigestion or who get drunk do not know how to eat or drink.

10. **Un dessert sans fromage est une belle à qui il manque un œil.** A dessert without cheese is a beautiful woman missing one of her eyes.

TOP TEN Famous Lines of Poetry

1. **Mais où sont les neiges d'antan?** Where did time go? Where are the snows of yesteryear? (François Villon, *Ballade des femmes du temps jadis*)

2. **Je suis le Ténébreux,—le Veuf,—L'Inconsolé.** I am the dark, brooding one, the widower, the unconsoled. (Gérard de Nerval, *El Desdichado*)

3. **Les parfums, les couleurs et les sons se répondent.** Perfumes, colors, and sounds respond to each other. (Charles Baudelaire, *Correspondances*)

4. **Là tout n'est qu'ordre et beauté, luxe, calme et volupté.** There, all is order and beauty, luxuriousness, calm, and sensuous delight. (Charles Baudelaire, *L'Invitation au voyage*)

5. **O saisons, ô châteaux. Quelle âme est sans défaut?** Oh seasons, oh castles. What soul is without fault? (Arthur Rimbaud, *O saisons, ô châteaux*)

6. **De la musique avant toute chose.** Music above all. (Paul Verlaine, *Art poétique*)

7. **Il pleure dans mon cœur comme il pleut sur la ville.** It weeps in my heart as it rains on the town. (Paul Verlaine, *Il pleure dans mon cœur*)

8. **Sous le pont Mirabeau coule la Seine.** Under the Mirabeau bridge flows the Seine. (Guillaume Apollinaire, *Le Pont Mirabeau*)

9. **C'était un bon copain.** He was a good buddy. (Robert Desnos, *C'était un bon copain*)

10. **Comprenne qui voudra.** Understand if you like. May anyone who wants to understand be able to. (Paul Eluard, *Comprenne qui voudra*)

TOP TEN Improvisations from Quotations

1. **Des goûts et des couleurs, on ne discute pas.** You can't argue with personal taste.
Des coups et des douleurs, on ne discute pas. Blows and pains are not to be discussed. (Coluche)
2. **Partir, c'est mourir un peu.** To leave is to die a little.
Partir, c'est crever un pneu. To leave is to get a flat tire. (Coluche)

3. **Rien ne sert de courir, il faut partir à point.** It's no use running to catch up, you need to start on time.

   Ce n'est pas tout de mourir, il faut mourir à temps. It's not just a matter of dying, you have to die in time. (Sartre)

4. **Une fois n'est pas coutume.** Doing something just once doesn't matter.

   Une foi est coutume. Faith is a habit. (Prévert)

5. **Plus on est de fous, plus on rit.** The more the merrier.

   Plus on aide le fou, plus on rit. The more you help the madman, the more fun it is. (Prévert)

6. **Il y a loin de la coupe aux lèvres.** There's many a slip twixt the cup and the lip.

   Il y a loin de la route aux escargots. There's a good distance between the road and the snails. (Eluard)

7. **L'espoir fait vivre.** Hope keeps people alive.

   L'espoir fait vivre mais comme sur une corde raide. Hope keeps you alive, but as on a tightrope. (Valéry)

8. **L'Etat c'est moi.** I am the state.

   L'éclat c'est moi. I am the sparkle. (an advertisement for diamonds)

9. **Aide-toi, le Ciel t'aidera.** The Lord helps those who help themselves.

   Aide-toi, Contrex t'aidera. Help yourself and Contrex will help you. (a slogan for Contrex mineral water)

10. **Mieux vaut tard que jamais.** Better late than never.

    Mieux vaut arriver en retard qu'en corbillard. Better to arrive late than in a hearse.

Rehearsal Time

Create new sayings (serious, comic, or surrealistic) from the following expressions by changing one or more words or by adding to them. Choose five expressions to experiment with.

1. Mieux vaut tard que jamais.

2. C'est en forgeant qu'on devient forgeron.

3. Rien ne sert de courir, il faut partir à point.

4. Aide-toi, le Ciel t'aidera.

5. Partir, c'est mourir un peu.

6. Paris vaut bien une messe.

7. L'argent ne fait pas le bonheur.

8. Je pense donc je suis.

9. Comment peut-on être persan?

10. Dis-moi ce que tu manges, je te dirai ce que tu es.

Complete the following quotations in the original version and then create a new expression. The originals are all included in this chapter.

11. L'hypocrisie est

12. Petit poisson

13. Le cœur a ses raisons

14. Sous les pavés

15. On n'est pas née femme

Write a few personal definitions in French loosely using any of the following models. Some possible concepts to be defined: *le malheur*, *l'ambition*, *la passion*, *la haine*, *l'argent*, *la beauté*, *la vérité*, *oublier*, *écrire*, *réussir*.

16. Bonheur: faire ce qu'on veut et vouloir ce que l'on fait.

17. L'hypocrisie est un hommage que le vice rend à la vertu.

18. Dis-moi ce que tu manges, je te dirai ce que tu es.

19. Tout comprendre, c'est tout pardonner.

20. Qui ne dit mot consent.

Ten Tricks and *Trucs*

In this section you cope with the tricks of French by reducing each complicated problem to a manageable form.

Le système D

When you follow *le système D* you figure out your own way of handling a confusing situation. The *D* of *le système D* stands for *se débrouiller*, to manage (literally, to get out of *le brouillard*, "the fog"). If you are *débrouillard* or *débrouillarde* you know your way around.

Se débrouiller is a tricky verb. Some of the uses you hear most are *Débrouillez-vous! Débrouille-toi!* "Figure it out for yourself!" *Il/Elle se débrouille.* "He/She always manages somehow." *On va se débrouiller.* "We'll figure out how to cope."

The Present Instead of the Future

In spoken French you frequently use the present tense to mean the future. This is partly just because the future tense is used much less often in conversation than in writing, and partly because the future isn't used the same way in French as it is in English. In French you can't use the future for the immediate future. The immediate future always has to be expressed with *aller* in the present tense. *Vous allez voir des exemples* can be translated "You're going to see some examples" and "You'll see some examples." You can also express a slightly uncertain future by saying *Vous devez les voir bientôt* to mean "You'll see them soon."

When you do use the future in spoken French, you tend to use it in ways that you wouldn't in English. We've seen that you say *Vous m'écrirez?* as the train is pulling out of the station as a request meaning "Don't forget to write!" You could add *Et tu n'oublieras pas de mettre la lettre à la poste?* "And don't forget to mail the letter!"

And in French you would have to use the future to say *Quand j'aurai le temps!* meaning "When I have time!"

In the following situations, the French avoid the future in situations where it's used in English. The first six sentences use verbs in the present tense. The last four are in the immediate future tense, formed with *aller* in the present.

TOP TEN   Examples of Getting Along Without the Future Tense

1. **Elle arrive tout de suite.** She'll be right there.

2. **Ils se marient l'été prochain.** They'll get married next summer.

3. **Est-ce que je dois rester?** Shall I stay?

4. **Je le fais?** Shall I do it?

5. **Voulez-vous le faire, s'il vous plaît?** Will you do it please?

6. **Demain matin, ils vont au marché.** Tomorrow morning they'll go to the market.

7. **Ils vont le finir tout de suite.** They'll finish it right away. (Or, they're going to finish it right away.)

8. **Je vais faire la sieste.** I'll take a nap. (Or, I'm going to take a nap.)

9. **Je vais rendre visite à des amis.** I'll visit some friends. (Or, I'm going to visit some friends.)

10. **Je vais faire une visite à ma grand-mère.** I'll go see my grandmother. (Or, I'm going to go see my grandmother.)

Subjective Subjunctives

The bad news about the French subjunctive is that there are many complicated rules. The good news is that you don't need most of the rules in order to use it correctly in informal French conversation.

Sometimes the main point about the subjunctive gets overlooked. The subjunctive involves a subjective attitude, a particular coloring of reality from a personal perspective. This becomes apparent in expressions such as *Je suis désolé(e) que nous soyons en retard*. Regret about being late colors the fact of being late. *Nous sommes en retard* is just a fact. "We're late."

Consider the following ten pairs of sentences:

TOP TEN Ways to Show a Subjective Perspective

1. **C'est le meilleur film que je connaisse.** It's the best movie I know. (It's just your opinion. You're subjective.)
   C'est le plus haut bâtiment que j'ai vu. It's the highest building I've seen. (The height has been measured. You're objective.)

2. **Elle ne croit pas que ce soit vrai.** She doesn't believe it's true. (She has her doubts, so maybe it isn't true.)

   Elle croit que c'est vrai. She thinks it's true. (And it probably is.)

3. **Je cherche quelqu'un qui puisse le faire.** I'm looking for someone who might be able to do it. (It's not clear whether such a person can be found.)

   Je cherche quelqu'un qui peut le faire. I'm looking for the person who can do it. (And in fact I know just the person who can do it.)

4. **Je suis désolé que nous soyons en retard.** I'm sorry we're late.

   Nous sommes en retard. Désolés. We're late. Sorry.

5. **Il est possible qu'on soit treize à table.** There may be thirteen of us at the table. (It's uncertain.)

   Il est probable qu'on sera treize à table. There will probably be thirteen of us at the table. (That's what you can expect.)

6. **Connaissez-vous quelqu'un qui sache le faire?** Do you know anyone who might know how to do it?

   Connaissez-vous quelqu'un qui sait le faire? Do you know someone who knows how to do it? (There are people who know how to do it. Do you know one of them?)

7. **On n'est pas sûr que ce soit vrai.** We're not sure it's true.

   On est sûr que c'est vrai. We're sure it's true.

8. **Nous emballons son cadeau avant qu'elle n'arrive.** We're wrapping up her present before she gets here. (She's not there yet.)

   Nous avons emballé son cadeau après qu'elle était arrivée. We wrapped up her present after she arrived.

9. **Je ne pense pas qu'ils viennent.** I don't think they're coming. (It's uncertain.)

   Je pense qu'ils vont venir. I think they're going to come.

10. **Je doute qu'il ait dix-huit ans.** I doubt he's eighteen.

    Il a dix-huit ans. He's eighteen. (There's no doubt about it.)

The Everyday Subjunctive

The subjunctive is rarely used in English, but it's used in everyday conversation in French. It makes sense to concentrate on being able to use the basic expressions of French conversation before going on to practice the more scholarly points that you'll rarely if ever need when speaking. Here are some frequently used expressions that are followed by the subjunctive.

J'ai peur que	I'm afraid (that)
Je suis content que	I'm glad (that), happy (that)
Je veux que	I want
Il est possible que	It's possible (that)
Je ne crois pas que	I don't think (that)
Je doute que	I doubt (that)
Il faut que	It's necessary that
Je suis désolé(e) que	I'm so sorry that
Il semble que	It seems that
Connaissez-vous quelqu'un qui	Do you know anyone who

The sentences below provide everyday examples of the verbs *avoir* and *être* in the subjunctive.

TOP TEN Common Uses of the Subjunctive in Conversation

1. **J'ai peur que nous soyons en retard.** I'm afraid we'll be late.

2. **Je suis content que tu sois parmi nous.** I'm glad you're here with us.

3. **Je veux que ce soit un succès boeuf.** I want it to be a great success.

4. **Il est possible qu'elle soit malade.** It's possible that she's sick.

5. **Je ne crois pas qu'ils soient amis.** I don't think that they're friends.

6. **Je doute que tu aies trop chaud.** I doubt you'll be too hot.

7. **Il faut que nous ayons de quoi vivre.** We have to have enough to live on.

8. **Je suis désolé(e) que vous n'ayez pas de réponse.** I'm sorry you're not getting an answer.

9. **Il semble qu'ils aient raison.** It seems that they're right.

10. **Tu connais quelqu'un qui ait un ouvre-boîte comme ça?** Do you know anyone who has a can opener like that?

Add a New Meaning with *en*: *Ne vous en faites pas!*

You are familiar with the pronoun *en* from expressions like *J'en ai*, "I have some." In some cases, *en* has become part of a verb, creating a new meaning and a new expression. A good way to get used to the pronoun *en* is to learn it in the context of whole expressions such as the following. These expressions serve as a reminder that language is in evolution.

Note the contrast between the following pairs:

prendre	to take
s'en prendre à	to blame
se moquer de	to make fun of
s'en moquer	to not give a hoot,
	to blow something off
faire	to do
s'en faire	to worry

sortir	to go out
s'en sortir	to manage to get out of a difficult situation
remettre	to put off
s'en remettre à	to leave up to (someone else)
tenir	to hold
s'en tenir	to set a limit, to hold to
tirer	to pull
s'en tirer	to get out of a difficult situation
vouloir	to want
en vouloir à quelqu'un	to be angry, have it in for someone
finir	to finish
en finir	to get something over with
venir	to come
en venir	to be after something, to be driving at something

TOP TEN Idioms with *en*

1. **Il s'en prend à ses amis maintenant.** He's laying into his friends now, blaming them.

2. **Je m'en moque.** I couldn't care less.

3. **Ne vous en faites pas. (Ne t'en fais pas.)** Don't worry. Don't get upset.

4. **Je ne vois pas comment on va s'en sortir.** I don't see how we're going to manage.

5. **Ils s'en remettent à vous/toi.** They leave it up to you.

6. **Je m'en tiens là.** I'll leave it at that.

7. **Il s'en est bien tiré.** He did well with a difficult job.

8. **Elle m'en veut.** She's mad at me, resentful of me.

9. **Il faut en finir.** Let's get it over with.

10. **Je vois où vous voulez en venir. (Je vois où tu veux en venir.)** I see what you're driving at.

Add a New Meaning with *y*: *Vous pouvez vous y faire!*

The pronoun *y* usually replaces a place. *J'y vais* is "I'm going there." *Y* could be *en France* or *à Paris*. *J'y vais* would work for going anyplace, and can also just mean "I'm leaving." In the following expressions *y* is more along the lines of the *y* in the sentence, *J'y pense*, "I'm thinking about it." It creates different meanings. Compare these pairs of verbs with and without *y*.

faire	to make
s'y faire	to get used to
perdre	to lose
s'y perdre	to get lost, to find confusing
prendre	to take
s'y prendre	to go about doing something
manquer	to miss
y manquer	to fail to do something

renoncer	to renounce
y renoncer	to give up
compter	to count
y compter	to count on
tenir	to hold
y tenir	to count on
retrouver	to find again
s'y retrouver	to find oneself in the same situation
reconnaître	to recognize
s'y reconnaître	to get one's bearings
ne pas s'y reconnaître	to feel completely lost
répondre	to answer
y répondre	to correspond to an idea, to meet requirements

TOP TEN Idioms with *y*

1. **Il ne peut pas s'y faire.** He can't get used to it.

2. **On peut facilement s'y perdre.** It's very confusing.

3. **Je m'y prends mal.** I'm not going about it the right way.

4. **Je ne vais pas y manquer.** I'll definitely do it.

5. **Il va falloir y renoncer.** We're going to have to give up.

6. **N'y comptez pas.** Don't count on it. (*N'y comptez pas trop.* Don't bank on it.)

7. **Nous y tenons beaucoup.** It's very important to us. We're counting on it.

8. **On s'y retrouve comme avant.** We're back in the same old situation.

9. **Je ne m'y reconnais pas.** I can't make heads or tails of this.

10. **Je ne sais pas comment y répondre.** I don't know how to answer.

Un coup

Some expressions just take longer to say in French. For example, "I nodded" would be *J'ai dit oui de la tête*. "I shook my head" would be *J'ai dit non de la tête*. That's the way it tends to be with the *coup* family. *Je lui ai donné un coup de pied* means "I kicked him" and *Je lui ai donné un coup de poing* is "I punched her."

Some of the expressions with *coup* were included in Tune-Up 8. Here are some more.

TOP TEN Kinds of *coup*

1. **Elle m'a donné un coup de pied.** She kicked me.

2. **Donne un coup de klaxon.** Honk.

3. **Elle est entrée en coup de vent.** She breezed in.

4. **Elle lui a fait un coup de tête.** She gave him/her a head butt. She acted impulsively toward him/her.

5. **Elle y a jeté un coup d'œil.** She glanced at it.

6. **C'était le coup de grâce.** It was the death blow.

7. **Il donne un coup de canif dans le contrat.** He has an affair from time to time.

8. **Ils ont subi des coups durs.** They went through hard times.

9. **Boire un petit coup, c'est agréable.** It's nice to have a little drink. (line from a song)

10. **Vous avez un bon coup de fourchette.** You like to eat.

Les faux amis

Un faux ami, "a false cognate," is a tricky French word that looks like an English word but has a different meaning. Sometimes *un faux ami* has a *double* meaning like the word *exciter*, "to excite," that can suggest in French that you're aroused by desire. Or maybe you unwittingly call someone *un bon homme* (*bonhomme*), thinking you're giving a good person a compliment when you're really implying that you don't take him seriously.

Les faux amis can lead you to talk about *un caractère*, a temperament or personality, as if it were a character in a book, when you mean *un personnage*. Or you might say *actuellement*, "now," when you mean *vraiment*, "actually."

Some of these *faux amis* lend themselves to embarrassing misunderstandings.

les préservatifs	condoms
Condom	a French town
un agent de conservation	a preservative (for cooking)
la confiture	jam, preserves
coucher	to go to bed with someone (or simply to spend the night)
se coucher	to go to bed

baiser	to fuck (slang)
un baiser	a kiss
un bachelier	a recipient of the baccalaureate diploma
un (une) célibataire	a single person, an unmarried person
la luxure	lechery
le luxe	luxury
une licence	a diploma similar to the B.A. degree
une licence	license, freedom used with irresponsibility, licentiousness
un permis de conduire	a driver's license
être pleine (enceinte)	to be pregnant (literally, full)
être grosse	to be pregnant (fat)
avoir bien mangé	to have eaten well (to be full)
attendre un enfant	to be pregnant
attendre ses enfants	to wait for one's children
les affaires	business
les affaires du cœur	personal, sentimental matters
une aventure	an affair (or an adventure)
un bonhomme	a poor old fellow (condescending when not used to refer to a child)
un homme très bien	a good man

TOP TEN Potentially Embarrassing *faux amis*

1. **Cette confiture contient un agent de conservation?** Is there a preservative in this jam?
   Où sont les préservatifs, s'il vous plaît? Where are the condoms, please?

2. **Ils se couchent comme les poules.** They go to bed early (like the hens).
   Ils couchent ensemble. They're sleeping together.

3. **Il m'a donné un baiser.** He gave me a kiss.
   Il baise bien. He's a good fuck.
   Il a été baisé. He got fucked over.

4. **Mon oncle est célibataire.** My uncle is single.
   Il est bachelier. He passed the baccalauréat (exam). He graduated from high school.

5. **Elles aiment le luxe.** They like luxury.
   La luxure, c'est un des sept péchés capitaux. Lechery is one of the seven deadly sins.

6. **Elle a son permis de conduire.** She has her driving license.
   Il est tombé dans la licence. He lapsed into debauchery.

7. **J'ai bien mangé.** I ate well. I've had plenty to eat.
   Je suis pleine. I'm pregnant.

8. **J'attends mes enfants.** I'm waiting for my children.
   J'attends un enfant. I'm pregnant. I'm expecting a baby.

9. **Quant à ma femme, les affaires vont bien.** As for my wife, her business is going very well.
   Ce n'est pas son affaire. It's none of his or her business.
   Ils ont eu une aventure. They had an affair.

10. **C'est un petit bonhomme de cinq ans.** He's a little five-year-old child. (*Un bonhomme de neige* is a snowman.)
    Il est bon. He's good. (moral, charitable)
    Il est très bien. He's a nice, decent person.

More *faux amis*

Actuellement ("currently") is not "actually" and *éventuellement* ("possibly") is not "eventually." With so many words spelled the same way or similarly in French and in English, you have to watch out for all sorts of *faux amis* among the *vrais*. The following false cognates may not lead to embarrassing situations in the same way as words like *la luxure*, but they will, nevertheless, lead you astray unless you're wary. *Il m'a injurié* means "He insulted me." *Vous me faites injure* means "You wrong me," while *Vous me blessez* means "You're injuring me." (*Soyez béni* is "Bless you" in a spiritual sense—but *Ah, toi, je te bénis* is "Damn you!") Watch out in particular for the following verbs:

injurier	to insult
blesser	to injure, to hurt someone's feelings
défendre	to forbid or to defend (depending on context)
justifier	to defend or justify one's actions or opinions
prétendre	to claim, to say something is true
faire semblant	to pretend
embarrasser	to get in the way
gêner	to embarrass
commander	to order
donner des ordres	to command
ordonner	to arrange, to order
rester	to stay
se reposer	to rest

assister à	to be present at
aider	to assist, to aid
ignorer	not to be aware of
ne pas tenir compte de	to ignore, not to notice
passer sous silence	to ignore, not to mention
retourner	to go back to a place you've been to before
revenir	to go back to the place you started from
quitter	to leave a place or a person
démissionner	to quit, resign

(TOP TEN) Words to Watch Out For

1. **Elle l'*a injurié* parce qu'elle était très en colère.** She insulted him because she was very angry.

2. **Je te *défends* de sortir avec lui.** I forbid you to go out with him.

3. **Il *prétend* que c'est vrai.** He claims it's true.

4. **Je vois que tous ces livres vous *embarrassent*.** I can see that all these books are getting in your way.

5. **Nous avons *commandé* un repas.** We ordered a meal.

6. **Ils vont *rester* à la maison.** They're going to stay at home.

7. **J'ai *assisté* au cours.** I went to the class.

8. **J'*ignore* ce qu'elle lui a dit.** I don't know what she said to him/her.

9. **Je *suis retourné(e)* à ce restaurant parce que c'était bon.** I went back to that restaurant because it was good. (went back another time)

10. **Je dois vous *quitter* maintenant.** I have to leave you now.

Expressions with Two Verbs

Here are some two-verb combinations where the second verb is always in the infinitive (when they are used together) and the two verbs together have a special meaning.

The quotation, *J'ai failli attendre* is attributed to Louis XIV. Louis XIV was said to worry that he might be kept waiting. Usually everything was ready for him long in advance. So when his carriage was ready on time he complained *J'ai failli attendre*, "I almost had to wait."

- **J'ai failli tomber.** "I almost fell." *J'ai failli* is literally something along the lines of "to miss or to fail." It tends to be used in expressions like *Il a failli se faire écraser*, "He almost got run over." It's usually about just missing some major or minor catastrophe.
- **Avoir beau dire.** *Vous avez beau dire* means that you can say that all you like but it won't change anything. Talk is cheap. It's easy to say that, but it won't happen. *Avoir beau...* is "to do something in vain." *J'avais beau essayer, je ne réussissais pas.* "I could try as much as I liked, I didn't succeed." *Beau* in this case has nothing to do with beauty, although originally it had to do with having the right weather. Even when the weather was propitious, things didn't turn out as hoped.

Most of the verbs in the following two-verb combinations are not as tricky as *J'ai failli tomber* and *Vous avez beau dire*. It's just a matter of getting used to what they mean in combination.

- **Savoir faire.** More familiar perhaps as a noun than as two verbs, this started out as just two ordinary verbs: to know and to do. Then the two verbs linked up as *savoir-faire*, a noun that means know-how in French and manners in English. *Savoir* can be used with other verbs for knowing how to do things. *Savoir nager*, to know how to swim. *Savoir lire*, to know how to read. *Savoir écrire*, to know how to write. *Savoir jouer aux cartes*, to know how to play cards. *Ils savent très bien faire la cuisine* is "They really know how to cook."

- **Laisser faire.** More familiar in English as "laissez-faire," the economics doctrine, *laisser faire* is to let someone do something: *laisser parler, laisser dormir, laisser entrer*.

- **Faire faire.** This, on the other hand, is to get someone else to do something: *faire réparer*, "to get something fixed"; *faire nettoyer*, "to get something cleaned."

- **Vouloir dire.** This phrase most often appears in the question, *Qu'est-ce que ça veut dire?* "What does that mean?" (literally, to wish to say).

- **Penser écrire.** When used with another verb, *penser* can mean that you're planning to do something, not just thinking. *Je pense lui écrire* means you're intending to write to him or her. *Je pense y aller.* "I'm planning to go there." *Je pense partir bientôt.* "I'm planning to leave soon." Or at least I'm intending to. *Penser faire* is somewhere between thinking about doing something and having a definite plan.

- **Dire comprendre.** *Dire comprendre*, like *penser écrire*, leaves out a few words. *Je pense écrire* is *Je pense que je vais écrire. Il dit comprendre* is *Il dit qu'il comprend.* "He says he understands." "He says *that* he understands." Similarly, you can say *Il croit pouvoir le faire*, "He thinks he can do it."

- **Voir danser.** You can say both *J'ai vu danser ces danseuses*, "I saw those dancers dancing," and *J'ai vu danser ce ballet*, "I saw that ballet (danced)." With *écouter chanter*, you can say *J'ai écouté chanter ce chanteur*, "I heard that singer sing," and *J'ai écouté chanter cette chanson*, "I heard that song (sung)."

- **Envoyer promener.** This means "to get rid of someone" (literally, to send to walk). *Ils l'ont envoyé promener*, "They told him to get lost." *J'ai envoyé promener tous mes cahiers*, "I tossed out all my notebooks."

TOP TEN Examples of How to Put Two Verbs Together and Make Sense

1. **J'ai failli tomber.** I almost fell down.

2. **Vous avez beau dire.** That's easy for you to say.

3. **Elles savent nager.** They know how to swim.

4. **Laissez-la dormir.** Let her sleep.

5. **Elle l'a fait faire par sa mère.** She got her mother to do it.

6. **Qu'est-ce qu'il voulait dire?** What did he mean?

7. **Je pense écrire à ma sœur.** I'm planning to write to my sister.

8. **Il dit comprendre de quoi il s'agit.** He says he knows what it's all about.

9. **Ce sont les gens que j'ai vus danser.** Those are the people I saw dancing.

10. **Il l'a envoyé(e) promener.** He sent him/her packing. He got rid of him/her.

Things That Take Longer to Say in French

In French, more than in English, there is a tendency to use abbreviations (as seen in Quick Fixes and Tune-Up 7); to convey a lot in a few words (as seen in Tune-Up 3); and to contract syllables, words, and expressions (as seen in Tune-Up 7).

There's also a famous tendency for French to go in the other direction: to use more words to say something that's said with just a word or two in English. One example seen already is the use of the verb *aller* in expressions such as *aller à pied*, "to walk"; *J'y vais à pied*, "I walk there"; *aller en voiture*, "to drive"; *On va y aller en voiture*, "We're going to drive there." Sometimes cultural differences are at the origin of these longer expressions. For example, *faire des courses*, "to do errands," has come to mean just "to shop." Shopping for food in France often involves going to many small shops, such as *la crèmerie* ("the cheese shop, the dairy") and *la charcuterie* ("the delicatessen, the butcher's shop"). The French continue to use the expression *faire des courses* even when all of the "errands" are done at the same *supermarché*.

It can work both ways. *Composer un numéro*, "to dial," is longer in French than in English, but *décrocher*, "to pick up (the receiver)," and *raccrocher*, "to hang up," are just one word each in French.

It's important in expressing yourself in French not to assume that a verb in English will be replaced by a single verb in French, and not to think that a particular structure in English will be identical to the structure in French. Otherwise you might miss out on an expression such as *dormir à la belle étoile*, the basic way of saying "to sleep outside." The following French expressions have shorter counterparts in English.

entrer sur la pointe des pieds	to tiptoe in
(marcher sur la pointe des pieds	to tiptoe)
montrer du doigt	to point
hausser les épaules	to shrug
dire oui de la tête	to nod
jeter un coup d'œil	to glance, to take a look
prendre sa retraite	to retire
faire ses valises	to pack
faire une demande d'admission	to apply
composer un numéro	to dial
coucher à la belle étoile	to sleep outside

TOP TEN Things That Take Longer to Say in French

1. **Je vais entrer sur la pointe des pieds pour ne pas la réveiller.** I'm going to tiptoe in so as not to wake her up.

2. **Ne montrez pas du doigt.** Don't point.

3. **Il s'est contenté de hausser les épaules.** He just shrugged.

4. **Elle a dit oui de la tête.** She nodded.

5. **Je ne l'ai pas vu mais je vais jeter un coup d'œil.** I haven't seen it but I'll take a look.

6. **Je vais prendre la retraite dans quelques années.** I'm going to retire in a few years.

7. **Nous faisons nos valises parce que nous partons demain.** We're packing because we're leaving tomorrow.

8. **J'ai fait une demande d'admission mais il va falloir attendre pour voir ce qui arrive.** I applied but I'll have to wait to see what happens.

9. **Après avoir composé le numéro, vous entendrez le bip sonore.** After dialing, you'll hear a tone.

10. **En été nous aimons coucher à la belle étoile autant que possible.** In summer, we like to sleep outside whenever possible.

Idioms and Variations

As you have seen throughout this book, you have to avoid literal translation from English if you want to speak real French. French has its own way of saying things. In the first model below, you say *J'ai faim* to mean "I'm hungry," but if you translated it literally, it would be "I have hunger." *J'ai mal au cœur*, "I feel sick," would be word-for-word "I have pain to the heart." But it's not even about your heart; it's what you say when you feel nauseous.

A note on *savoir* and *connaître*, two verbs that are famous for being confused. *Connaître* is for knowing a person or for knowing a place or thing on a personal level. *Savoir* is for knowing a fact, having some kind of general knowledge, or for knowing how to do something. *Savoir* does not always have to be followed by a second verb in the infinitive, the way it's used in the model, *Je sais conduire*, "I know how to drive." You can, of course, use other models, *Je sais que c'est vrai*, "I know it's true," and *Je sais l'adresse*, "I know the address." You can't use *connaître* with an infinitive, however. For this reason, the best and quickest way to get the hang of the difference in meanings between *connaître* and *savoir* is to learn a contrast in structure along with the contrast in meaning.

The following idioms will make your French grow exponentially. In each case you'll start with a familiar expression and go on to some that may be new to you.

TOP TEN Idioms and Their Variations

1. **J'ai faim.** I'm hungry.
   Ten variations: *J'ai soif* (I'm thirsty); *J'ai chaud* (I'm hot); *J'ai froid* (I'm cold); *J'ai sommeil* (I'm sleepy); *J'ai le temps* (I have time); *J'ai envie d'y aller* (I'd like to go there); *J'ai besoin de le faire* (I have to do it); *J'ai les cheveux bruns* (I have dark brown hair); *J'ai un rhume* (I have a cold); *J'ai quatre-vingt-quinze ans* (I'm ninety-five years old).

2. **J'ai mal à la tête.** I have a headache.
   Ten variations: *J'ai mal au cœur* (I feel sick); *J'ai mal aux dents* (I have a toothache); *J'ai mal aux pieds* (My feet hurt); *J'ai mal au ventre* (I have a stomachache); *J'ai mal à la gorge* (I have a sore throat); *J'ai mal aux oreilles* (I have an earache); *J'ai mal partout* (I'm aching all over); *J'ai mal aux cheveux* (I have a hangover). And with *le mal*: *J'ai le mal de mer* (I'm seasick); *J'ai le mal du pays* (I'm homesick).

3. **Je suis en avance.** I'm early.
   Ten variations: *Je suis en retard* (I'm late); *Je suis en colère* (I'm angry); *Je suis en panne* (I've run out of gas, something's broken down, or I'm stumped); *Je suis en bonne santé* (I'm in good health); *Je suis en pyjama* (I'm in my pajamas); *Je suis en deuil* (I'm in mourning); *Je suis en congé sabbatique* (I'm on a sabbatical); *Je suis en vacances* (I'm on vacation); *Je suis en tête-à-tête* (I'm having a private converation); *Je suis en ville* (I'm in town).

4. **Je vais en France.** I'm going to France.
   Ten variations: *Je vais au Sénégal* (I'm going to Senegal); *Je vais aux Etats-Unis* (I'm going to the United States); *Je vais aux Antilles françaises* (I'm going to the French West Indies); *Je vais à Paris* (I'm going to Paris); *Je vais à la campagne* (I'm going to the countryside); *Je vais dans le Massif Central* (I'm going to the Massif Central); *Je vais à l'école* (I go to school or I'm going to school); *Je vais à l'église* (I go to church or I'm going to church); *Je vais chez un(e) ami(e)* (I'm going to a friend's house); *Je vais chez le médecin* (I'm going to the doctor's).

5. **J'y vais à pied.** I'm walking there. (going on foot)
   Ten variations: *J'y vais à vélo* (I'm going to bike there); *J'y vais à cheval* (I'm riding there); *J'y vais à moto* (I'm going by motorcycle); *J'y vais en voiture* (I'm driving there); *J'y vais en train* (I'm taking the train there); *J'y vais en métro* (I'm taking the subway there); *J'y vais en bus* (I'm taking the bus; *en car* for a longer distance); *J'y vais en taxi* (I'm taking a taxi); *J'y vais en avion* (I'm going by plane); *J'y vais en bateau* (I'm going by boat).

6. **Je fais du sport.** I do sports.
   Ten variations: *Je fais de la natation* (I swim); *Je fais du tennis* (I play tennis); *Je fais du vélo* (I bike); *Je fais du jogging* (I jog); *Je fais du roller* (I rollerblade, do in-line skating); *Je fais de l'athlétisme* (I run track); *Je fais de la gym* (I work out); *Je fais de la voile* (I sail); *Je fais de la marche à pied* (I go for walks); *Je fais des randonnées* (I hike).

7. **Il fait beau.** It's nice out.
   Ten variations: *Il fait du soleil* (It's sunny); *Il fait chaud* (It's hot); *Il fait du vent* (It's windy); *Il fait mauvais* (The weather's bad); *Il fait gris* (It's overcast); *Il fait frais* (It's a little chilly); *Il fait froid* (It's cold); *Il fait du verglas* (It's icy; There's ice on the

roads); *Il fait jour* (It's daylight; It's daytime); *Il fait nuit* (It's nighttime).

8. **Je joue au hockey.** I play hockey.
   Ten variations: *Je joue au baseball* (I play baseball); *Je joue au football* (I play soccer); *Je joue au golf* (I play golf); *Nous jouons au chat et à la souris* (We're playing cat and mouse); *Je joue aux cartes* (I play cards); *Je joue au bridge* (I play bridge); *Je joue aux échecs* (I play chess); *Je joue à qui perd gagne* (I'm playing winners/losers); *Je joue aux boules* or *Je joue à la pétanque* (I play "boules," bocci, bowls).

9. **Je connais Jacqueline.** I know Jacqueline.
   Ten variations: *Je ne connais qu'elle* (I know her better than anyone); *Je le connais de vue* (I know who he is, I'd recognize him); *Je connais un bon hôtel* (I know a good hotel); *Je connais Paris* (I know Paris); *Je connais ce livre* (I know this book); *Je connais les insectes* (I know a lot about insects); *Je connais mon métier* (I know how to do my job); *Je connais mon affaire* (I know what I'm talking about); *Je connais la chanson* (It's the same old thing); *Je ne connais pas mon bonheur* (I don't know how lucky I am).

10. **Je sais conduire.** I know how to drive.
    Ten variations: *Je sais nager* (I know how to swim); *Je sais jouer du piano* (I can play the piano); *Je sais écouter* (I know how to listen); *Je sais attendre* (I know how to be patient); *Je ne sais quoi faire* (I don't know what to do); *Je ne sais quoi dire* (I don't know what to say); *Je sais le faire* (I know how to do it); *Je sais plaire* (I know how to be charming); *Je sais me défendre* (I know how to take care of myself); *Je sais m'y prendre* (I know how to go about it).

Answer Key

Tune-Up 1: Nonverbal Cues, Sound Effects, and Interjections

1. a pout

2. a pout with a shrug with the elbows close to the body and hands palms-up

3. forehead taps with the index finger

4. a lower eyelid pulled down with the index finger

5. three or four shakes of the hand from the wrist

6. *la bise*, a kiss on each cheek

7. a light handshake, up and down once, then release

8. pretending to write on the palm of one hand with the other hand

9. making a telephone with your hand, thumb and little finger extended, and bringing your hand to your ear

10. stroking your chin and rolling your eyes

11. Aïe!

12. Zut!

13. Hein?

14. Pchch!

15. Euh...

16. Bis!

17. Youpi!

18. Ouste!

19. Beurk!

20. Chiche!

Tune-Up 2: Manners

1. Bonne soirée!

2. Bonne nuit!

3. Bonne santé!

4. Bon courage!

5. Bonne année!

6. Bonjour, madame.

7. Bonjour, Monsieur l'Agent.

8. Bonjour, Madame la Directrice.

9. Bonjour, Madame la Ministre.

10. Bonjour, Docteur.

11. b

12. a, b, or h

13. e

14. f

15. g

16. h

17. i

18. j

19. d

20. c

Tune-Up 3: Idioms to Go

1. Attention!

2. Courage!

3. Doucement!/Silence!

4. On peut y aller en voiture.

5. On fait ce qu'on peut.

6. On est mardi.

7. Ici on parle français.

8. Je descends./Vous descendez?

9. J'écoute.

10. Je regrette.

11. J'arrive.

12. Je réfléchis.

13. Tant mieux.

14. Il a mauvais caractère.

15. Ça tombe bien.

16. Vous avez bonne mine.

17. Vous avez tort.

18. Ça m'ennuie.

19. Je m'en vais.

20. Elle est difficile à vivre.

Tune-Up 4: Practical French

1. aller (aller-retour)

2. seconde

3. wagon (wagon-restaurant)

4. composter

5. quai

6. douche

7. cour

8. grand

9. parking

10. compris

11. regarde

12. qui

13. salon d'essayage

14. combien

15. Comptant/Carte bleue

16. l'appareil

17. quittez

18. passe

19. ligne

20. rappeler

Tune-Up 5: Table Talk

French Table Manners (page 100)

1. d

2. a, d

3. a, b, c, d. Stick to water or wine.

4. a, d. The French think that water should not be too cold. Therefore, no ice cubes. And some consider Perrier too fizzy to be served with meals.

5. a. *La tulipe* lets the wine breathe.

6. a, b. Some topics that you consider acceptable may be considered rude in France. Of course, it depends on whom you're with. The meal should be a pleasant occasion, a respite from the day's activities.

7. b, d. *Les mains sur la table* is an old rule. Both hands should be seen at all times.

8. b. When there's a bread-and-butter plate, you use it, but you won't usually be given one unless you are at an elegant restaurant.

9. b. Perhaps this is because French spoons are bigger than American ones.

10. c

11. a

12. c

13. a

14. d. Don't specify a dressing unless asked. It's the chef's job to choose the right dressing.

15. b, c. You're not supposed to cut lettuce with a knife.

16. c, d, f

17. b

18. a. The main thing is for the knife and fork to be together and parallel.

Le repas (page 107)

1. a, c. A heavier wine such as *porto* would be served after the meal.

2. a. The French don't go in much for appetizers. A few nuts or biscuits, *les amuse-gueule*, may be served before the meal.

3. b. The first course, *les hors d'œuvre*, is served at the table.

4. a, b. There are several variations on this in France. In the United States the entrée is the main course. Usually in France *l'entrée* is served before the main course, but it's sometimes used to mean the main course.

5. b. If you see something called *le plat*, it's the main course.

6. b. Salad, lettuce with vinaigrette, is served after the main course. Otherwise *la salade* would be a salad with a special

name such as *salade niçoise* and it would not be served after the main course. *Les crudités*, raw vegetables such as carrots, radishes, and cucumbers, may be served at the beginning of the meal.

7. a. The salad is usually just lettuce with vinaigrette after the main course.

8. b. Cheese should always be accompanied by wine, but wine doesn't have to be served with cheese. Cheese is said to interfere with the appreciation of the best wines.

9. c. Breakfast is the only meal that you have *with* coffee. Otherwise, coffee always comes after the meal, and it will be espresso. Milk is not offered with coffee after lunch or dinner.

10. b. The meal may be followed by a liqueur, which should be sniffed and then sipped slowly.

Rehearsal Time

Possible answers:

1. Qu'est-ce que vous me proposez? Un kir/un lillet/un dubonnet, s'il vous plaît.

2. Avec plaisir./Volontiers./Merci. Pas de champignons.

3. Avec plaisir./Volontiers./Merci. C'était délicieux.

4. Il se fait tard. Il est temps de rentrer. (If you want to stay you can say *Si. On peut rester une petite minute.*)

5. C'est très gentil si ça ne vous dérange pas trop./Non merci. On a la voiture.

6. On est deux./On est trois. (If you are alone you can say *Je suis seul(e)*.)

7. Sur la terrasse, s'il vous plaît./A l'intérieur.

8. Moi, je prendrai le melon de Cavaillon/le jambon de Bayonne/les champignons farcis...

9. Quelles sont les spécialités de la maison?/Quelles sont les spécialités de la région?/La brandade de Nîmes./L'agneau à la provençale./Le cassoulet.

10. Qu'est-ce que vous me recommandez pour accompagner cela?/ Du blanc./Du rouge./Un vin du pays, s'il vous plaît./(or a particular choice)

11. La tarte aux pommes./Le clafoutis./Merci. Pas de dessert.

12. Un déca, s'il vous plaît./Un express.

13. les vins blancs secs

14. les grands vins

15. le champagne

16. le vin blanc sec

17. un vin doux ou le champagne

18. un rosé

19. Il est long en bouche. Il est souple et léger. C'est un vin mûr.

20. C'est du picrate. Il est dur et un peu acide. Il est imbuvable. Il tourne au vinaigre.

Tune-Up 6: Conversation Starters

Possible answers:

1. Comment peut-on y aller?

2. Combien de temps faut-il pour y aller?

3. Où est-ce que je dois descendre?

4. Est-ce que c'est loin?/C'est loin?

5. Où est-ce que je peux garer la voiture?/Où est-ce que je peux stationner la voiture?

6. D'où venez-vous?

7. Quelle est votre situation de famille?

8. Que faites-vous dans la vie?

9. Quel est votre numéro de téléphone?

10. Quelle est votre adresse e-mail?

11. Quelle est votre adresse?

12. Quel parti politique vous intéresse?

13. Vous avez des projets pour demain?

14. Est-ce que je pourrais vous accompagner?

15. Est-ce que vos parents vivent toujours?

16. Dans quelle ville française vit-on le mieux?

17. Quel est le plus beau paysage de la France à votre avis?

18. Quelle est la plus belle cathédrale française à votre avis?

19. Les Français élèvent-ils bien leurs enfants?

20. Quelles sont les fêtes françaises les plus importantes?

Tune-Up 7: Slang and Other Kinds of French

1. a

2. b

3. b

4. b

5. a

6. c

7. b

8. a

9. c

10. b

11. a

12. a

13. b

14. c

15. c

16. b

17. c

18. b

19. b

20. a

Tune-Up 8: Attitude

1. b

2. c

3. a

4. a

5. b

6. b

7. c

8. a

9. a

10. b

11. le trou normand

12. dans le pétrin

13. le pied de grue

14. un poil dans la main

15. pour mieux sauter

16. des gorges chaudes

17. le coup de foudre

18. dans ses petits souliers

19. à la lune

20. je-m'en-foutiste

Tune-Up 9: Wit

1. Pas mal.

2. Ce n'est pas tous les jours fête.

3. Elle ne manque pas de culot.

4. Ce n'est pas facile.

5. Ce n'est pas évident.

6. Ce n'est pas exclu. Ce n'est pas la mer à boire.

7. Ce n'est pas donné.

8. Ce n'est pas de la petite bière.

9. Elle n'est pas bête.

10. Il n'est pas brillant. Il n'a pas inventé la poudre.

11. a

12. c

13. c

14. a

15. c

16. Etienne

17. Alice

18. Alonzo

19. Auguste

20. Alphonse

Tune-Up 10: Improvisation

Answers will vary.

Index of Top Ten Lists